Baseball Comes Hon

The Magic of Raley Field and the Sacramento River Cats' Premiere Season

Created and Edited by

Bob Androvich with Will James

Photographs by Bob Solorio

ARTISTS	**DESIGNERS**	**PHOTOGRAPHERS**	**WRITERS**
Steve Barbaria	Jennifer Pechette	Ben Androvich	Bob Androvich
Lisa Carpenter	Circus Catch Publishing	Toni Cordero	James L. Burton
Carl Chiara		Gordon Lazzarone	Jeff Caraska
Bob Dahlquist	Tackett-Barbaria Design Group	Jim Lynn	Doug Curley
Eric Decetis	Design Consultants	Maggie McGurk	Ed Goldman
John W. Hansen		Bill Prince	Diana Griego-Erwin
Jolene Jessie		Bob Solorio	Will James
David Lobenberg		Jay Spooner	Mark Kreidler
Dan McAuliffe		John Tessler	and
Nan Roe		Monica Turner	Poet Laureate
Stephanie Taylor		Bob Van Noy	Viola Weinberg
Mary Lynn Tenenbaum			
Ed Weidner			

Edited by Bob Androvich
Designed by
Jennifer Pechette of Circus Catch Publishing
Design consultation by
Tackett-Barbaria Design Group
Cover illustration by Steve Barbaria
Composed by Jennifer Pechette and
Bob Androvich of Circus Catch Publishing

Printed in Sacramento, California by
Graphic Center

Contributor copyright information is listed on
pages 94 and 95.

Library of Congress
Cataloging-in-Publication Data

ISBN 0-9640859-0-9

Androvich, Bob
James, Will

Baseball Comes Home
The Magic of Raley Field
and the Sacramento River Cats' Premiere Season
Bob Androvich
Will James

Please make all inquiries to:
Circus Catch Publishing
P.O. Box 19410
Sacramento, CA 95819
online @ www.CircusCatch.com
Phone toll-free 1-877-335-0779

Acknowledgements

Like the success of Raley Field, *Baseball Comes Home* is a result of a monumental team effort. I was lucky to be the GM, director of player personnel and manager of the team and owe thanks to everyone who suited up for Circus Catch Publishing this past year.

First, the new heroes of the region: Art Savage, Bob Hemond and Warren Smith. Without their vision, perseverance and guts, we'd still be refusing to attend Steelhead games. They went out on a limb and allowed me to create the book. I will be forever thankful for their gracious support and cooperation.

Will James, my co-author, offered endless inspiration, creativity and dedication to the project. His copious notes and astounding memory are the backbone of the book. Together we attended most of the games (he missed just two!) and his passion for the sport refreshed mine.

Kristy McAuliffe, my partner at Circus Catch, kept a diligent eye on the business while Will and I deserted the office for Raley Field. I couldn't hope for a better "podnah."

Kim Tackett, Steve Barbaria, Gaye Rowley and Pam Matsuda of Tackett Barbaria Design Group stepped up to the plate to format the book, a monstrous task. Their incredibly generous donation of time, staff, and patience gave the book its gorgeous look and feel.

The artists, writers and photographers who made contributions deserve special thanks: all of them jumped aboard the project on a leap of faith. Thrilled by the return of professional baseball, all were eager to join the team. I doff my hat to Lisa Carpenter, Jeff Caraska, Carl Chiara, Toni Cordero, Doug Curley, Bob Dahlquist, Ed Goldman, Diana Griego-Erwin, John W. Hansen, Jolene Jessie, Gordon Lazzarone, David Lobenberg, Jim Lynn, Nan Roe, Stephanie Taylor, Mary Lynn Tenenbaum, Bob Van Noy, Ed Weidner and Viola Weinberg. Extra credit must be paid to Bob Solorio and Jay Spooner, photographers who were always there when I needed their time and talents. Their skills bring the magic of Raley Field to life in *Baseball Comes Home.*

Thanks to all of our friends in the River Cats organization and at Raley Field. In the front office, Gary Arthur, Tom Glick, Bob Herrfeldt and Dave Wolloch opened doors for us all season. Mike Gazda always made us feel welcome in the press box. Tony Asaro, Brian Thornton and Darrin Gross were constantly there on the concourse to make things easier for us. Dinger, Daren Giberson, Raffi Siegel, and Doug Berrios kept us laughing. Brian Farley's clubhouse tour was a season highlight. Kristi Goldby and her army of Guest Services charmers made every visit to the ballpark an absolute delight.

Mike Vinks, Tag Gebhart and Gary Ordway from J. R. Roberts Construction made sure we got complete access to the construction site, all the while keeping us from being run over by heavy equipment.

The fans at Raley Field made this project the best "job" I've ever had. Every game, Will and I couldn't wait to "go to work" to meet and talk with the wonderful, friendly, diverse people that poured through the gates. Always ready to talk or pose, Raley Field fans were outgoing, cheerful and helpful.

And I can't forget the people in the background, always ready to help: Everyone at Walgreen's 1-Hour Photo (at Arden and Eastern); Brownie's Documat; and Graphic Center. Their professional, timely service ensured we met our tight deadline.

Most Valuable Player for the year arrived late in the project: Jennifer Pechette—graphic designer/office manager–assembled the entire project. If there's a "star" in the lineup, it's got to be her.

And last, but not least, I must thank my wife, Teresa, and kids, Ben, Joe and Mary. Their constant support, encouragement and assistance granted me the time to make *Baseball Comes Home* a labor of love.

DEDICATION: This book is dedicated to the memory of Dan McAuliffe.

Baseball
COMES HOME

Table of Contents

The Magic of Raley Field

The River Cats' Premiere Season

Baseball Comes Home

Introduction   by Bob Androvich

The return of minor league baseball to Sacramento was inevitable, a given. For years, I believed warm summer nights at the ball yard were just a matter of the right people and the right place colliding with good timing.

I believed Fred Anderson would pull it off in 1994, but the place (the concrete bunker in place at Arco Arena) didn't work. I believed Gregg Lukenbill had a chance at the same site, but the people and place didn't pan out.

In 1997, after Fred passed away, Bob Hemond and Warren Smith came to me with their vision to bring Triple-A Baseball to West Sacramento

and I BELIEVED! Their perfect mix of people, place, and timing convinced me these guys would bring their dream to fruition. Their site was perfect for a ballpark, their integrity was unblemished and their timing was as good as it could get. As the competition between the three groups battling to bring baseball back to Sacramento heightened, community interest in minor league ball grew with it, and when these two unassuming, straight-up guys delivered their dream on paper, who could not believe in their vision? When Art Savage arrived and added a team, fresh capital, and incredible sports marketing savvy to the vision, Bob and Warren's dream melded into reality.

River City Baseball had a team, they had obtained financing for their ballpark, and just over eight months to have the yard ready in time for Opening Day.

I was convinced it was the story of the year in Sactown and I wanted to be the one to tell it. Within hours of the approval to begin construction, I was pounding on Bob's office door, practically begging for the project. Minutes later, I was on the job at "The Triangle" dodging bulldozers and earthmovers, shooting pictures.

And here we are, a year later. In that magical year, Art, Bob and Warren delivered to us the 1999 Triple-A Champion Vancouver Canadians, created an organization 700 strong that caters to every guest's taste, whim, and need, and placed them in a ballpark that inch-for-inch rivals any other (at any level) in the nation: Raley Field. And to top it all off, the River Cats pounded their rivals, posting a 90-54 record, with an incredible 48-19 record at their new home.

Baseball Comes Home is about this past year, how belief turned to reality, and reality turned to magic. An unbelievable premiere season built on belief. Bob and Warren's belief. Art's belief. OUR belief that it was just a matter of time until baseball came home.

Then and Now

Since the Sacramento Solons departed the circus-like atmosphere of Hughes Stadium after the 1976 season, the Central Valley ached for the return of legitimate professional baseball.

The Pacific Coast League and Triple-A baseball had left and it seemed like the game would never come back.

The 70s ended and the 80s passed and although a number of runs were made at bringing baseball back home to Sacramento, every attempt fizzled. In the early 90s it was obvious that baseball would someday return, and the big question was what level of baseball.

Politicians hopped on their bandwagons and proclaimed Sacramento a "major league" city worthy of a major league team. When a number of groups began to seriously pursue minor league baseball as a less expensive, more realistic alternative, it took a couple of years to convince local fans that "the minors" were a worthy substitute.

Some area fans had experienced Single-A baseball at California League games in Stockton and Modesto. A few had traveled out of state to see Triple-A action, since the top level minor league had completely deserted California. But for most area fans, their minor league experiences and memories harkened far back to the 1950s, the Sacramento Solons and Edmonds Field.

In the days before the big leagues expanded to the West Coast, the Pacific Coast League was huge. Packed with dozens of major league-quality players who, for one reason or another, chose to stay "out west," the PCL clubs included Hollywood, San Diego, Oakland, San Francisco, Seattle, Portland, and Sacramento. Edmonds Field, the last in a series of ball yards constructed on the southeast corner of Broadway and Riverside Boulevard, was home to the Solons from 1945-1960.

As River City Baseball's Pacific Coast League team-without-a-name made their plans for the premiere 2000 season, most Sacramentans couldn't get over the Solons and Edmonds Field. Many felt the team should (no matter what!) be named the Solons—even if they didn't know what a Solon was! Those same fans also longed for Edmonds Field—with its left field line bleachers, knot-hole gang, wooden outfield fences—to somehow magically reappear for this "new team" in West Sacramento.

What the Sacramento region got was the River Cats and Raley Field. Pacific Coast League, Triple-A baseball, with a new, bold, brazen identity—not the Solons—and arguably the best new ballpark in America—not Edmonds Field!

Raley Field—brought to you by an incredibly talented and conscientious ownership; managed and operated by an all-star cast of vice-presidents and directors; and delivered every night by one of the very best customer service organizations, anywhere.

And Minor League Baseball—the show most of the fans had no idea they were buying: mascots, non-stop entertainment, distractions for the kids, cool players coming up, players going down.

Once the doors opened and fans—even the hard-core Solons fans—entered Raley Field, it became crystal clear: the Solons and Edmonds Field—that was then. The River Cats and Raley Field—this is now.

The Dream

Baseball comes home, on warm summer evenings, drawing starved fans from far and wide, "minor league ball and major league fun" set in a jewel of a ballpark, nestled on the West Sacramento riverfront with one of the best views in the sport.

JOHN W. HANSEN

After a condensed, Cinderella-story season at magical Raley Field, it's difficult to imagine any other scenario. But if it hadn't been for the persistence of Bob Hemond and Warren Smith, fans could be watching Single-A games in a concrete bunker amid the barren horizons of Arco Arena.

The magical story of how Hemond and Smith teamed up with Art Savage and a Dream Team of regional movers and shakers has been told: Two young, baseball-mad Sacramentans jump start a new regionalism with the return of Triple-A baseball to the "other side of the river," West Sacramento. They did it! The good guys won. In the classic "American way:" via thorough preparation, hard work and tireless determination, Hemond and Smith made their dreams—and ours—come true.

The fairy tale ending didn't come easily, and there were some very bad days for the lads. Savage's experience helped. In a textbook case of "been-there-done-that," his cool demeanor helped get his partners through one of the worst days. "There had been a grueling, all day, late night meeting with West Sacramento officials," said Hemond, and both sides went back and forth over numerous issues. Near midnight, officials announced the deal was off. "They said, 'We just can't do it. Good night,' Hemond recalled. Stunned, the three partners went home. The next morning, Hemond and Smith showed up at the office, suffering from a sleepless night of worry and anxiety.

"Art drove up and bounced into the office, obviously well rested and calm," Smith said. "I looked at Bob and we looked at Art and said, 'What's the deal, Art? We were up all night worrying. What are we going to do? How could you sleep?'"

"I slept like a baby," replied Art. "I took NyQuil".

The Dream Team

Bringing baseball back to Sacramento was a daunting task and would not have happened (especially in such a short time) without a Dream Team roster of regional corporate partners, politicians, and loyal, dedicated citizen supporters that shared The Dream.

"Mike Teel gets my vote as MVP," declared Hemond. Smith added, "At the time, Mike wasn't a baseball fan, but he knew what Raley Field would do for the community." Teel, president and chief executive officer of Raley's, believed in The Dream right off the bat.

"Roger Dickinson ranks right up there with Michael," Hemond states. "Roger immediately understood how important this project was for the region." Dickinson, long-term member of the Board of Supervisors, pledged his support early on, when it was politically incorrect to do so. Dickinson helped create the Joint Powers Authority, an alliance of the County of Sacramento, City of West Sacramento, and Yolo County.

"The real MVP of the 'Dream Team' was Art," Smith concludes. "The only thing 'Minor League' here is the game–all the rest is major league all the way," Smith says, "and Art was responsible for that."

Savage himself nominates Frank Ramos. Ramos, businessman, real-estate developer and uncrowned king of West Sacramento, stepped in a number of times to convince key players to stay on track and not give up on The Dream.

Christopher Cabaldon, West Sacramento mayor, was another early believer. He joined the Dream Team and made the return of baseball to West Sacramento the city's top priority.

Muriel Johnson gave River City Baseball their war cry. At a JPA press conference, Dickinson was taking a beating from reporters. The diminutive Johnson strode up to the podium, nearly brushed Dickinson aside and stated: "One little river can't stop baseball, and one little river can't stop us from joining forces."

"From that moment on, most everyone supported the project," Hemond notes.

Mike McGowan, Yolo County supervisor and former mayor of West Sacramento, coined the concept of "the river as Main Street." That concept was stressed time and again as The Dream began to "suddenly" come true.

The first "Dream Team" player made everything else possible. Beverly Walton owned "The Triangle," the site Smith felt was the keystone of their plan. "Baseball rules say that the batter's eye must face northeast," Smith said, "and this site was perfect for what we envisioned. Beverly owned it."

Walton smiles, remembering their first meeting. "There was this young man parked in his truck on the property," she says. "I walked over to it, and tapped on his window." Smith rolled the window down, and was about to speak. "I'm sorry sir, but this is private property, and you are trespassing!"

"She was ready to throw me off the property!" Smith recalls. Smith told her of The Dream, then what he could offer her for the parcel. Soon, the coveted "Triangle," the first bit of magic, belonged to Hemond and Smith. Within a year, "The Dream Team," working along countless parallel tracks, would bring baseball back home to Magical Raley Field.

Dream Team members at the Raley Field Groundbreaking Ceremony October 28, 1999 (left to right): Rob Siebers of Sacramento Coca-Cola; Loretta Walker of Pac Bell; Warren Smith; Art Savage; Joyce Raley Teel; Michael Teel; Roger Dickinson; Mike McGowan; Christopher Cabaldon; Tom Stollard; Helen Thompson, California State Assembly; Muriel Johnson; and Bill Kristoff.

Thomas P. Raley

In the 1970s, "Mr. Raley and I stood on the west bank of the Sacramento River," said former Raley's president and CEO Chuck Collings, "on property covering three blocks. Above us was the Tower Bridge. Across the river we could see the Capitol and Capitol Mall. Mr. Raley dreamed of people enjoying both sides of the river, walking back and forth over a great archway, hopping on board river taxis to visit shops and restaurants and hotels along the waterfront." Raley put his money where his dreams were: he built his corporate headquarters in West Sacramento, and created Raley's Landing on the west bank across the river from Old Sacramento. Although a baseball field wasn't exactly what Tom Raley envisioned, Thomas P. Raley Field would have suited him just fine!

Michael Teel, Raley's grandson who succeeded Collings as CEO, committed the supermarket chain to a 20 year naming-rights-partnership with River City Baseball, convinced that Hemond and Smith's vision fit perfectly with his grandfather's. Most rewarding to Teel is witnessing families making the trek across the river to enjoy a new, wholesome source of entertainment. It's only a matter of time until Tom Raley's full-blown vision comes true.

Raley Field

While The Dream Team spread out on their parallel tracks of action, Joe Diesko and Greg Prelager of HNTB Architects were on a high-speed track of their own: the design of Raley Field.

"We showed them five or six sites the first time they were here," said Smith, "and we didn't tell them we favored Beverly's parcel." The next day, Diesko and Prelager returned with their one and only choice: The Triangle. Its northeast facing orientation, immediate proximity to the Tower Bridge, unrivalled view of the Sacramento skyline, and easy accessibility all combined to make it the perfect site for a ballpark. Rebar-bending construction deadlines forced the architects to keep just a couple of drawings ahead of J.R. Roberts Construction, the general contractor, and their army of subcontractors.

Design quality usually suffers under such a critical deadline, but from the first discussions and sketches, it was obvious Raley Field would be an exception. Taking cues from the Tower Bridge, its web-steel trusses echo the 1935 landmark. Savage is credited with insisting on the extra-wide, spacious concourse around the seating bowl. The height of the concourse was also raised to create an even more airy, fan-friendly area. Viewing areas for disabled fans, complete with power outlets, were set on the concourse at the back of the seating area.

"The Dream Team" knew Raley Field would be done on time. Diesko and Prelager knew it could be built on time. J.R. Roberts knew they would build it on time. But, as late as Labor Day, 1999, the site was still littered with derelict warehouses, and the talk of the town was, "Will they get it built on time?"

Parallel Tracks
Out of Dreamland

Most of the public focus was on Raley Field and whether it would be done in time for opening day, but in the background much, much more was happening at River City Baseball. One hundred parallel tracks led out of the offices and the site.

Savage went on a hiring rampage, building a front office twice the size of the average minor league club. What he didn't bring from Vancouver, he found. What he didn't find, came to him. "For 20 years, my philosophy has been to hire the best people you can find," Savage says. "And I did." Each vice president was given his track, and the directors who reported to them were given their own trains.

Gary Arthur, the vice president and general manager of the ballclub, moved to Sacramento with the team from his native Vancouver, where his efforts brought the city the Triple-A championship. Arthur's job was to move the team and prepare for spring training.

Tickets went on sale. Dave Wolloch was recruited from the San Francisco Giants by Savage to get sales moving. The first day on the job was a big surprise for Wolloch. "Art, Warren and Bob's office was in a beatup old shack on the site," Wolloch fondly remembers. "They had a card table and a phone set up for me at one end. That was it."

Bob Herrfeldt, vice president of stadium operations, was recruited by Savage as well. When Herrfeldt showed up at "the office," he made his wife wait in the car. "I wondered, 'Oh man, what have I got myself into?'"

Tom Glick, vice president of sales and marketing, came to Raley Field to "put on the show." The focus of each person, on each track, was intense. "It was like, keep moving, or get out of the way!"

Dan Vistica, vice president of finance and administration, another Savage find, was charged with keeping track of all of the money that would be moving around. "It was like eating an elephant–one bite at a time," Vistica recalled.

Kristi Goldby was brought on board to hire, train and supervise a staff of 140 Guest Services recruits. "We conducted 300 interviews a week," Goldby said.

And to top it all off, a new partnership was formed between Raley's and River City Baseball, to provide all food and beverages at the ballpark. Would creating a new, vertically integrated food service business distract the ever-expanding Dream Team? No. It was just one more track out of dreamland.

A Construction Miracle

From the moment the earthmovers cranked over their engines to Opening Day was just eight and a half months. Considering the increased liability, sensitivity, and litigious direction the construction industry has taken, that is a miracle.

But like everything else associated with The Dream, people came together to do whatever they could to make it come true. To construct a facility on such a high-speed track required extraordinary levels of trust, confidence, and teamwork among the hundreds of people who made it happen. Art Savage elaborates: "I had known Dan Vistica for 27 years. Dan put together a golf game with Larry Nurse, COO of Raley's, and Bob Olsen, co-owner of J.R. Roberts Construction." That round of golf was the foundation for the owner-contractor agreement.

A spring-like fall enabled J. R. Roberts Construction to proceed full speed ahead. Crews worked from sunrise to sunset. On other sites, heavy-pressure construction with subcontractors working in such tight quarters, can erupt into shouting matches and occasionally into fisticuffs. But not at Raley Field: a "whistle-while-you-work" atmosphere settled over the site.

"When we would visit the site," Smith recalls, "the workers would tell us what a great place this would be."

Fall turned to winter and dirt turned to concrete. Structural steel went up at the end of the year. April 14th seemed like years away. Raley Field was taking shape. On the street, a conversation between two fans went like this: "I went out to Raley Field yesterday," said the first, "and is it going up quickly!" "It had better," was the reply.

And then it rained. And rained. And record amounts of rain. On Raley Field, on the schedule, on the deadline. The deluge prompted the move of Opening Day back to May 15th. Luck fell on The Dream, for when the deluge was over, the rain was gone, pretty much for good.

Crews went back to work en masse, feverishly slaving to meet the deadline. Workers labored

through a two-day open house held a few days before Opening Day. Seat numbers and signage were still being installed and electricians and technicians toiled into the nights-fixing this, adjusting that-as fans swirled through "their" new gem of a ballpark.

And then–absolutely ready or not–it was done. Finished. A construction miracle had indeed occurred and it was time to share that miracle with the thousands of baseball fans clamoring for a game. Bunting adorned the fences. A party tent filled the upper right field berm. Banners welcoming fans were hung over the gates. It was May 15th and finally Opening Day.

An 18-month project completed in eight-and-a-half months...

"Eating an elephant one bite at a time"
Dan Vistica

The "Triangle" begins to resemble a ballpark.

The seating bowl takes shape.

A rare "off" day.

Gaining a foothold and going up.

Sand lot.

Raley Field skywalkers.

The berm takes shape.

A full-scale erector set.

Last-minute details.

*Raising the roof
       at Raley Field.*

Turf is laid by the yard and ruined by the foot.

Art Savage—proud owner of a new ballpark.

I did that!

J.R. Roberts takes a bow for a job well done!

"Thank you, Mr. Raley"–

Liz Lentsch

'Raley Field in 10 Words or Less' – August 31, 2000

On Raley's Field

by Viola Weinberg

A lush mown lawn lies green-on-green in tartan check

Wrapped neatly on the shoulders of the mound—

White chalk ground along the lines, laced through long legs

Of the luscious diamond where runners slide and fielders shield—

Abundant, verdant greens, dazzling and fresh, perfume of grass

With swollen, flat beads of dew on earth precisely groomed

White bags of base, white rubber of mound for pitcher's foot

And the precious place with spindled roof that we call home.

The Magic Of Raley Field

Mag•ic \'maj-ik \ adj [ME *magik*,fr. MF *magique*, fr. L *magice*, fr. Gk *magike*, fem. Of *magikos* Magian, magical, fr, *magos* magus, sorcerer of Iranian origin; akin to Oper *mogush* sorcerer] **2 a :** having seemingly supernatural qualities or powers **b: giving a feeling of enchantment.**

A RECIPE FOR MAGIC

Mix together the return of baseball (in a semi-miraculous fashion); the game – including 85 players and a Cinderella-story season; amusing entertainment, good food and top-of-the-line merchandise; a first class, gracious, caring Guest Services staff ——— Pour ingredients into an absolutely perfect baseball park (one with an unrivalled skyline view works best) pre-filled to the brim with adoring fans. No cooking is required – magic will occur immediately (guaranteed).

The Magic of Raley Field first cast its enchanting spell on its subjects May 15, 2000–Opening Night. A thunderous deluge just hours before game time threatened to spoil the event famished area baseball fans had awaited for over 20 years. Groundskeepers covered the field; fans scurried for cover, opened umbrellas and hunkered down in the squall; party-goers on the berm squeezed together under a tent; Guest Services staff retreated to the concourse.

The massive, turbulent storm hung over Raley Field, bruised cotton candy clouds pouring rain on the River Cats' parade. And then it stopped. And went away. And did not come back. Had the "seemingly supernatural powers" of Raley Field chased off the weather? Were fans "given a feeling of enchantment?" Magic?

Yes. The Magic of Raley Field.

In a New Stadium, a Timeless Feeling

by Diana Griego-Erwin

OPENING DAY, Raley Field – It's seven hours before game time as Bob Herrfeldt stands behind home plate stifling a grin bigger than Montana.

In front of him, groundskeepers on riding lawn mowers etch a herringbone pattern into grass so green it shimmers. His cell phone rings constantly. In come needling last-minute questions about loose wires and squeaky turnstiles, the ones that can drive a guy crazy if he lets them.

Herrfeldt, the River Cats' vice president of operations, fields each question deftly. But through the Opening Day jitters, he never takes his eye off the ball, or what's really going to count days, weeks and years later: the feeling the area's baseball-crazy fans will experience the moment they step through the gates into their new ballpark.

Noon, and Herrfeldt's still not sure where he wants to stand when that moment comes. Down by the railing, watching fans spill down into the ballpark? Or maybe he'll stand at the front gate and tear that first ticket.

Men in business suits stroll over during lunchtime and peer in through the locked gates for a sneak preview. What is it about baseball? How to describe the feeling? Herrfeldt and a crew of hundreds built this dream and, yet, even he can't quite get his arms around the mystique of baseball's allure. His wife recently asked him to explain it and he fumbled for the words.

"I just don't know," he said Monday. "It's like that moment in 'Field of Dreams'… He says something like, 'Hey, Dad, do you wanna catch?' and you've been there. Something about throwing a baseball back and forth makes you think you're a dad, makes a son a son. There's just something."

When someone mentions the crack of the bat, a fan knows exactly what that sounds like. You can visualize the fluid way the third baseman will field and hurl the ball to make the out at first without even knowing who's starting. There's a precise way it must be done.

There are things that must accompany the experience. Peanuts. Hot dogs. Pennants. The seventh-inning stretch. Otherwise, it's not baseball.

Grown men will scrape their shins and jam their knuckles diving for foul balls just to prove to themselves they still have those Little League moves that once made their heart swell–and still do, so powerful and lovely are the memories.

A new generation of fast-pitch softball-throwing girls will watch the lucky nine on the field and say, "I can do that."

Young boys like the Brooks brothers from Elk Grove will look at the ballpark in wonder and awe and imagine playing there.

Brook Brooks, 8, remembers what it felt like to learn to slide, fear grabbing his heart, dirt flying everywhere. He loves the sound of people cheering.

His older brother, Brannon, 11, loves the exactness of the game, the rules, the finesse required in doing something right. He'll also be sizing up the River Cats for role models. Right now, Atlanta Braves third

baseman Chipper Jones is the man, but, hey, he's open.

The feared words "rain out" cloud everyone's day, but Herrfeldt's not sweating it. "It won't," he said of the rain. It's as if he's made a deal with the devil.

The heavens burst open at 5:29 p.m., one minute before the gates are set to open. Lance Lynch, a 12 year-old catcher with the Hangtown Cardinals, is the first ticket holder in the door. He hit his first home run Sunday and now this. "Baseball's great," he says, grinning. "Anything can happen."

Former San Diego Padres Rookie-of-the-Year Butch Metzger–an emergency medical technician at Monday's game–says baseball's kind of like life.

"There are changes, heartbreak, moments of pure joy. (Like life), you're having great success if you fail seven out of 10 times."

Young fans pound at the center of their gloves, ready for that first foul ball. Stadium employee Stan Smith, 75, says the game grabbed America's soul and never let go. "I guess it was better than milking cows or something."

A rainbow appears one hour before game time. "Play ball!" the ump finally yells and they do.

Baseball's back in Sacramento.

Matt LaRose's crew protecting hallowed ground.

Baseball's back in Sacramento.

This is May 15th! It's Opening Day—it can't rain!

Hard-core baseball fans are not to be denied.

Is Raley Field at the end of the rainbow?

Raley Field: Just Right For Triple A

by Mark Kreidler

Out in the five-dollar cheapies, along the rolling slope of grass beyond the left-field fence, the future of Raley Field was in full debate an hour before the first pitch had ever been thrown in the place.

Thoughtful Ed offered the obvious: "They'll get a chance to have a major-league team here in five years, seven tops."

Sarcastic Steven couldn't resist: "If we're outdrawing Oakland, wouldn't that be trading down?"

And West Sac Sid, a longtime resident who saw this little gem of a ballpark go up brick by beam in a place where constructing something of actual beauty seems almost inconceivable, managed to compress our scattered considerations into a single, pithy thought.

"They could expand it for the A's," Sid said, looking around. "God, I hope they don't."

Amen to that.

It was minor-league straight down the line Monday night, and that's good news. The River Cats christened Raley Field and brought back legitimate pro baseball to the Sacramento region for the first time in nearly a quarter-century; and almost against our better nature, we found ourselves hoping that this is it.

Triple-A baseball will work here, probably in a way that the big, expensive, corporate-soaked major leagues never could; and it took just a few trips around the Cat box to understand on how many levels that's true.

The tickets are right, the baseball is real. The stakes are relevant, if not overwhelming. It'll play.

And Raley Field is the place, a ballpark that manages to be brand new without actually seeming shiny. It is the special province of the minor-league park that what it mostly looks like is clean and sharp – not pyrotechnic on any regular basis, not the purveyor of steady sonic overhead.

Corny when it should be, affordable around the edges.

Just… about… right.

The players' own desperate fight to get to the major leagues duly noted, you've got to start with the proposition that this is, first and foremost, about having a good time. If you saw the families piling out of the place Monday at about the seventh-inning stretch, you know.

It's about getting in, seeing the sights, grabbing some chow and finding your way out in time for the kids to wake up for school the next morning. That's why Raley Field itself ultimately might matter more than A.J. Hinch or Ariel Prieto or whoever else happens to be wearing the uniform.

And we're happy to report that the park is up to all that. As former major-leaguer Butch Metzger, one-time Kennedy High star noted, "Sacramento just raised the bar for all other Triple-A franchises."

About the bad seats: We didn't find any. A walk around the park is a stroll past good sight line after good sight line, including the concourse level, which offers a fairly clean view down to field level as you make your way to the long, long concession lines.

You could make the argument that the folks who ponied up for the luxury suites actually have the inferior view, albeit the best food service. They're at the highest rise of the stadium structure. Everything else sits down below, and the look is all good.

The best deals, clearly, are the picnic areas beyond left and right field—and not just because they're cheap. On the turf-slope beyond left, you're positioned just about perfectly for a dead-pull right-handed hitter to send a ball screaming your way.

Over in right field, you look practically straight down on the side-by-side, home-visitor bullpens, the better to heckle.

Dinger mingles with Joint Powers Authority movers and shakers.

Anyone who comes to Raley Field, of course, will have a quibble. Our problem with the outfield retaining wall is remarkably basic: It doesn't have enough junk on it and there are no moving parts.

If you're in the minor leagues, you are constitutionally required to have a billboard with at least one moving part—a waving arm, a cow's tail, something. Raley does get points for featuring a "Hit It Here" bull's-eye above the 98 Rock sign in left field, but we'll be looking for the mechanical cup of steaming coffee any day.

A microbrew costs $5.50, and at the memorabilia stands we saw Raley Field t-shirts going for $21. Scandalous. On the other hand, you could yank a red rope away from a vendor for two bucks, thus calming your 6-year-old for at least four minutes.

And the best look, oddly enough, may be the one you never see inside. At the main entrance to the ballpark, the words "Raley Field" stand in huge, Coney Island-style midway lighting, beckoning you to come in and look around.

It's a totally minor-league look, which must be why it works. We'll go with West Sac Sid on this one: Triple-A, from where we stood on Monday, looked just about right.

Most members of 'The Dream Team' were on hand to toss out the ceremonial "first pitch" on Opening Night.

Baseball Comes Home: The official first pitch at the region's brand new ballpark.

The River Cat's out of the bag: Dinger makes his Opening Night debut!

Welcome Home

The "seemingly supernatural power" of Magical Raley Field was cast over those who passed through

its gates with an assist from the enchanting Guest Services army of over 100 people.

As the ballpark welcomed the national pastime back home, Guest Services welcomed the fans home—

with care, concern and best of all, with sincere joy and enthusiasm.

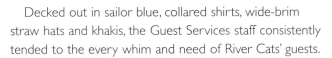

*Mark McComas with Sacramento Bee mascot, ScooBee (above);
Enthusiastic Guest Services staffers Jewel Carter (right); and Sally
McCoy (far right), made everyone feel right at home at Raley Field.*

Decked out in sailor blue, collared shirts, wide-brim
straw hats and khakis, the Guest Services staff consistently
tended to the every whim and need of River Cats' guests.
Guest Services director Kristi Goldby spearheaded the creation and training of the team. "We interviewed for over a month solid," Goldby says, a
staggering 300 interviews per week. "We had 10 rooms going at a time,"
Goldby recalls.

"People were beating down the door to work here," she says. "We were
lucky, because everybody we hired really wanted to work here. Half of
them probably would have worked for free."

The astounding level of customer service and attention to detail Guest
Services delivered every night was a result of an organization-wide com-
mitment. "Art Savage, Bob Herrfeldt and I all shared the same vision" of
the ideal customer experience. Eighteen hours of orientation and training
imprinted that vision to every Guest Services recruit.

Guest Services people were everywhere: the gates, berms, concourse,
aisles, stairwells and every door—ready to cheerfully bend over backwards
to help a fan. Jack DeGeorge and Esther Lopes greeted members of the
press, dignitaries and fans at their station near the elevator. A perpetually
full candy bowl for guests sprinkled sugar coating on their already-sweet
demeanor.

Jewel Carter usually could be found at the main gate, dispensing her joy
to ticket holders pouring into Raley Field, and then later spreading the
Raley Field gospel outside the merchandise store. Her impression of working at this magical site: looking heavenward, she sighs, "Take me to the stars!"

Win a prize? Turn in a survey? Just want to know what's up at Raley
Field? Chances are, you met Patsy Coleman or Lillian Townes, stationed at
the Guest Services kiosk behind home plate on the concourse. Coleman

and Townes, like all of their colleagues, always strive to go the extra mile—
"No problem!"—to insure a wonderful experience.

The magic of Raley Field extended to disabled fans like nowhere else in
baseball. Guest Services staff members greeted fans curbside at the main
entrance and escorted them to the special disabled seating areas on the
main concourse. When fans were ready to leave the spell of the ballpark,
Guest Services escorts were there to return them to the main parking lot
and their waiting transportation.

This extra special care and treatment of the fans represents and rein-
forces perhaps the most single endearing quality of the West Sacramento
fan-friendly franchise and its spell-binding facility—old fashioned hospitality;
arguably unrivaled by the staffs at any sport venue, whether they be Minor
or Major League in status.

"Little things," Goldby says, "the icing on the cake," like booster seats for
kids, helps cast that magical Raley Field spell. "You go anywhere right now,"
she says, "and you just don't get the service you used to—and I hate it!"

It's no wonder that the River Cats established an all-time PCL attendance record of 861,808 paying customers. Guest Service's "Welcome
Home" this season added personal charm to the already irresistible Magic
of Raley Field and enhanced every fan's experience each time they
returned. After all, the ultimate goal of Art Savage, Bob Herrfeldt, Kristi
Goldby and all their charges is to be able to greet fans with "Welcome
Back."

Guest Services Photo Gallery

Director of Guest Services, Kristi Goldby.

Ever-diligent in providing the finest baseball experience.

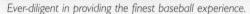

Patsy Coleman—always ready to help—with a big smile.

LaRae Shaw-Meadows and Holly Westervelt's charm rubbed off onto guests.

Sweet Marie McGregor kept suite ticket holders happy.

Rick Gallegos offers up a Guest Services smile.

Raley Field "In Seat Runner" Finny Moseley.

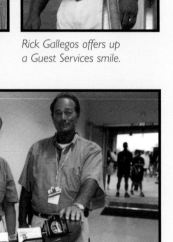

Jack DeGeorge and Esther Lopes and their famous bowl of candy.

"Fan Appreciation Night" at Raley Field.

Jewel Carter, "Queen of the Merchandise Store."

Matt LaRose's crew was the best!

Jennifer Perkins beamed up orders from fans to the kitchen.

Tony Asaro, Manager of Community Relations.

Val Mata spread his magic at Raley Field.

The right field berm crew pauses to say thanks.

Darlyn Redding surveying guest action from the bridge.

Luke Galbert... genuine friendly customer service.

Willie Williams always wore a bright smile at the ballpark.

Chris Dillion rakes the mound before a scorching day game.

Lillian Townes worked at various spots all season.

31

Eat—Drink—Gear Up— And Enjoy The Show!

Welcome over 12,000 guests to your home every night, satiate their palates, quench their thirsts, wow them with an endless array of entertainment, offer them souvenirs to remember their visit and then send them all home so completely thrilled with the evening that they will crave a return visit. That is Tom Glick's job with the River Cats.

Glick, vice president of sales and marketing and his well-oiled, talented staff put on "The Show" every night at Raley Field. Not the game—The Show—about everything *but* the game. "In order to open yourself up to the widest possible audience, you make it about the whole experience: the food, music, contests, the game, the players. It's a broad mixture."

Once through the portals of the ballpark, most fans head straight for the concession stands for their favorite ballpark meal. The barbecue on the right field outer berm packed in diners with delicious ribs and tri-tips. Giant "Dinger Dogs," hot roasted peanuts, root beer floats and other specialties elevated Raley Field's fare far above the commonplace "dogs-and-peanuts" available at the majority of minor league ballparks.

Next stop? Most likely, the merchandise store, or one of the many souvenir stands on the concourse. Like the concession stands, the store was usually packed with customers. "We offered high-quality products," Glick states, "and we kept things new—what the fans asked for." The River Cats sold more gear than any team in minor league baseball this year, as fans swept up caps, shirts, and other assorted mementos reminding them of the magic of Raley Field.

Minor league baseball's revival in the mid-80s was fueled by screwball, between-inning entertainment, and the River Cats dished up plenty to keep the fans howling and happy. Brian Thornton, director of marketing, says, "The Show is 75 percent of the experience in minor league baseball." Thornton and his staff (among other things!) coordinate the music, in-house broadcasting, promotions and on-field entertainment.

A state-of-the-art control room located dead center on the suite level provides Arlow Moreland the perfect vantage point to direct the show on game day. Working from a down-to-the-minute script, armed with a cell phone, two-way radio, headset and telephone, Moreland orchestrates the sound, video, and action in the ballpark, all the while electronically besieged by his legion of troops from all corners of the facility.

On-field entertainment was actually cut back soon after the season began. "Sacramento fans, are probably 50 percent baseball, only 50 percent show," Thornton says. "So, we backed off a bit and let the game breathe." But that "half show" provided plenty of entertainment for River Cats fans.

The newspaper toss, bat-spin race, kid's race around the bases, and karaoke were "between inning competitions" that got fans out of their seats, onto the field and into "The Show." Quite a treat, especially if they couldn't throw, run, or sing worth a hoot.

"The Famous Chicken" performed his now familiar (but still hilarious) act for the first time in Sacramento, to the crowd's absolute delight. The Blues Brothers blasted through Raley Field, driving their junker around the warning track, singing and dancing on the infield and then bounding up through the stands on the backs of seats.

Nobody got the crowd laughing as hard as "The ZooperStars," an odd assortment of inflatable rubber "mascots." When a walking basketball (visualize Pac Man) swallowed a bat boy and then proceeded to burp and spit out the batboy's uniform, piece by piece with every ensuing belch, 14,000 people went completely nuts.

The fan's favorite, though, was their own mascot: Dinger, the River Cat, and his nightly entrance on the Hot Dog Cannon (see feature, next page). His trips through the stands, dancing here, harassing there, melted through age barriers, and brought out the kid in everyone.

An astounding effort, by a mostly faceless crew enhances the fan experience at every River Cats game. From the kitchens, to the souvenir stands, to the control room, dedicated, talented "magicians" are doing their best to cast the spell of Raley Field upon us and have us long for more of The Show.

"It takes a lot of work. It amazes me every night when we pull it off," Thornton says. "I want to say it's a sense of relief, but it's…. satisfaction."

The Show—
A Night with Dinger and the Hot Dog Cannon

Game in, game out, one of the hardest working people at Raley Field isn't a Guest Services staffer or player. The hardest worker isn't even a person–it's Dinger, the River Cat: the team mascot. Dinger starts his day a couple hours before game time, when his "wrangler," Daren Giberson and other on-field entertainment crew members arrive at Dinger's Lair, and ends long after the last out of the contest.

"Okay, Dinger," Daren proclaims, "time to get up and go to work!" Dinger stirs and joins the crew, busily wrapping hot dogs for the nightly "Hot Dog Cannon" lap. The coveted hot dogs are carefully sealed in plastic bubble-wrap, complete with condiments and napkins, then launched a few hours later out of a CO2 powered cannon–enclosed in a four-and-a-half foot metal hot dog–from a groundskeeper's cart that speeds around the warning track. The Hot Dog Cannon is nearly as huge with the fans as Dinger.

In the middle of the first inning, Daren announces it's time to go, and leads Dinger out of the lair, to the clubhouse, via the first base line concourse. "Everybody loves Dinger," Daren says, as Dinger nods approvingly. "We've got to move quickly because once the kids see him…"

"DINGER!" screams a kid, the first to see the oversized mascot. Within seconds, he's surrounded: kids squeeze him, teenagers pound him, women kiss him. Every few yards, Daren stops to let parents take pictures of Dinger with their kids. Out the concourse, across the back of the right field berm, all the way to the center field gate, Dinger is swarmed by fans.

Minutes later outside the clubhouse, the Hot Dog Cannon Squad is assembled, armed, and loaded in their cart waiting for the last out in the top of the third. Dinger is sitting on the back deck of the cart with Daren,

who's in charge of loading the cannon, and "Tumbleweed," a clubhouse rat, who feeds Daren the "ammo."

"We've got some special ammo tonight," Tumbleweed tells Daren. "Some marshmallows, t-shirts and stuff." Brian Farley, River Cats clubhouse manager, is the wheelman. Raffi's the gunner. He's stationed behind Farley, half-sitting, half-standing, the cannon firmly in his clutches. The Squad is read–these guys love their job.

As the River Cats hustle to their dugout following the third out, the center field gate opens, and fan applause erupts into pandemonium as the cart turns sharply to the right, onto the left center field warning path and toward the stands. As the fans work themselves into a near-frenzy, Daren loads up a dog and, "BOOM!" Raffi sends it skyward, and as it slowly arcs down to outstretched arms of jumping fans… "BOOM!" another dog is blasted, and "BOOM!" another as the cart leaves the fans scrambling madly for the falling dogs.

Tumbleweed hands Daren a dog, then a t-shirt, then a bag-load of marshmallows. "BOOM!" As the cart passes the River Cats dugout, fifty marshmallows rain on the howling fans behind the screen. As Farley makes the turn behind home plate, Dinger is throwing hot dogs and assorted ammo to the folks in the first few rows.

The cart speeds out the right field warning track and the bedlam is complete: over 10,000 fans on their feet, jumping, shrieking–going absolutely nuts–for hot dogs. As the opposing pitcher digs in on the mound, the Hot Dog Cannon Squad makes a hard right turn through the center field gate, and out of sight–its mission accomplished: the crowd is in a lather.

Behind the fence, the Squad jumps off the cart, exhilarated from the minute-plus circuit. Dinger gives Raffi a huge high-five. Daren is in hysterics,

quizzing Tumbleweed. "Was that a banana you handed me?" Tumbleweed looks guilty, but Daren knows better. "Dinger?"

Dinger, hands behind his back, feigns a whistle, and attempts to look innocent. "Oh, boy," Daren scolds him, "are we gonna get in trouble for that!" But there's no time to yak: at the end of the inning, Dinger opens the center field gate, makes his entrance across the diamond and his first foray into the stands.

Out onto the field, Dinger quickly makes fun of an umpire, and then back into the stands he charges—looking for another victim. A middle-aged man, beer in hand, yells, "Hey Dinger!" and is covered with a blast of silly-string. Next? He bounds up the stairs about 20 rows and stops suddenly at the sight of a youngster who is obviously frightened of the River Cat. As Dinger nears, the young girl recoils into her dad's arm. Dinger slowly, gently, bends down and tenderly offers her his paw. Nudged by her dad, she shyly reaches out and reluctantly shakes hands with her new pal.

So much for tenderness. He's off again, up to the concourse and straight to the stairs leading to the suites. "Now we're really in for it," Daren moans. Dinger strides up to the first suite, and pounds as hard as he can on the closed door. The door quickly swings open, and a large, angry man begins to burst forth—who then sees Dinger—and melts into laughter.

The guests in the suite all love it as Dinger grabs a bottled water, strides past them to the outside balcony seats and begins to douse the fans below with its contents. Fans below squeal in surprise from the sudden shower as those upstairs cheer him on. He's on a roll and there's no way Daren, or any wrangler, could stop him now.

He turns suddenly and dashes out of the suite to another. He pounds on the door and another angry man yanks open the door—and there's

Dinger! Daren follows Dinger in and they head straight to the balcony. A two-foot spider, attached to a 30-foot elastic cord, is dangled off the balcony until it comes to rest on an unsuspecting fan's arm or head. Dinger's scaring the daylights out of people—and he's having fun.

Onward he moves, into the hallway leading to the third base line suites. Dinger picks up speed as he heads straight for the solid (and closed) double doors leading to the stairway back down to the concourse. Concerned guests in the hallway watch as he slams—with a huge crash—into the doors and collapses in a heap on the concrete floor.

Startled fans on the other side of the doors fling them open and there, lying flat as a pancake on the floor, is Dinger. One man nudges him gently in the side with his toe, but Dinger lies still as a stone. A lady bends down, ready to offer assistance to the fallen Dinger when he suddenly springs up—perfectly healthy—and scares the entire group nearly senseless.

Delighted with himself, he hops downstairs, two-steps it across the concourse and quickly moves into the stands behind third base. He proceeds to get the crowd clapping in support of the team, who are in the midst of clobbering the hapless visiting nine.

And on it goes. By the end of the night, it's a tired, beat—and happy–crew that reconvenes at the Lair, now transformed to Club Dinger. They recap the evening's show: what worked, what didn't, and share stories and laughs before heading home.

"It's long hours and low pay," says one of the crew, "but I wouldn't give this up for anything!" Dinger, Daren, Raffi, the Hot Dog Cannon Squad, they all agree. And their joy and enthusiasm is evident as a major ingredient in the recipe that makes the Magic of Raley Field.

"The Show" Photo Gallery

Harry Canary got the crowd crooning... "Take me out to the ballgame."

Raffi kept fans hopping between innings.

Steve Wall of the Beer Dawgs playing the national anthem.

The "Ball Toss"

Krazy George!

Raffi recruits a Guest Services member on Fourth Of July.

Doug leads the ostrich around the park.

The Chicken puts on one of the best shows of the year.

There's always something to entertain you... The Davis Junction!

Dinger, flanked by Jason DeMoss on left and Daren Giberson.

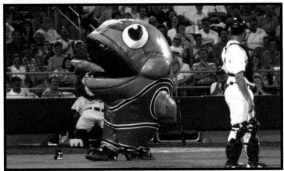

The 'Zooperstar' that swallowed (and then spit up) the bat boy, had 14,000 fans in hysterics...

A Night at the Ballpark

Magical Raley Field became a must-visit destination as soon as it opened.

Thrilled beyond expectations, guests left—the Raley Field spell cast upon them—and spread the word quickly: Raley Field was the place to be. Not just for the baseball—or "the show"—but, for what The Dream Team intended—a new regionalism.

Old Sacramento, normally "slow" on spring weeknights, sprang to life on game nights. "I think business will increase," said Michael Vaillancourt (above), managing-owner of Rio City Café, in April. Restaurateurs and merchants alike all anticipated more customers. Brett Shaffer of All American Sports Fan, an Old Town sports store, was excited: "The (River Cats' temporary) ticket office down the street has increased business,"

Shaffer said. "I know the ballpark will have a store, but they'll hopefully stop here first." Come August game nights, Rio City Café was impossible to get into without a reservation. With a grin from ear to ear, Vaillancourt could be found, running ragged, from 4:30 until late every evening the River Cats were at home. "Business could not get any better!" Shaffer agreed: "Foot traffic has jumped," Shaffer observed, "and so have sales."

Many Sacramentans made the trek from Old Sacramento or the Crocker Art Museum to Raley Field. "We eat in Old Sac before almost every game," Ray Reynoso, of Sacramento, said between bites at the Rio City Café. He and his friends park in Old Sac, then walk to the game. "It's a five minute walk," stated Reynoso. For many, it was the first time they had walked across (or even stood on) the Tower Bridge. Regional Transit shuttle buses ran every couple minutes on a regular downtown Sacramento route, ferrying fans across the bridge. The efficient, friendly jitneys offered fans priority curb-side drop-off as well. Free bicycle parking at Riske Lane and Ballpark Drive enticed cyclists to pedal to the park. For those driving to West Sacramento, access to "The Triangle" was smooth, with superb traffic control. With so many entrances to West Sacramento, gridlock was rare.

The most common compliment of Raley Field was, "There's not a bad seat in the house." And how true. Five-dollar seat on the grass? Perfect. Guest of a suite-owner? Oh yeah. Seats behind the plate? Wow! It really didn't matter where you sat: Raley Field was the best!

A night at the ballpark, with family or friends, reminded fans that baseball—done right—is the true national pastime.

Raley Field is just right day or night.

Fan's eye-view of right field berm beyond bullpens.

The setting sun casts a warm glow.

Raley Field Photo Gallery

The view from the Crocker Art Museum in "East" Sacramento.

A fisheye lens captures the full panorama of the berm.

The western horizon provides a beautiful backdrop for Raley Field.

Fireworks at the end of another charming night at Raley Field.

Minor league ballpark, major league scoreboard!

Warren Smith's view.

Quiet and beautiful Raley Field.

Dusk falls upon Raley Field.

Day or night, what a view!

A telephoto view of the berm and beyond.

"...The bombs bursting in air..."

Crowds were treated to a spectacular view and great baseball!

Pouring In

Baseball Comes Home. Indeed. All season long, dedicated fans were "pouring in" through the gates of Raley Field. For the final home game of the regular season, a beyond capacity crowd of 15,146 jammed in for "Fan Appreciation Night," establishing a new Pacific Coast League home attendance record of 861,808. In doing so, the River Cats also outdrew all the teams in the minor leagues.

During the regular season, Raley Field was officially sold out on 15 dates, with the final two sellouts topping the official capacity count of 14,111, and the last, exceeding 15,000. The River Cats averaged 12,312 at home—numbers that included four games played in Oakland before the completion of Raley Field. Had the Cats just drawn their average attendance at Raley Field for each of the Oakland games, they would have drawn more than 900,000 for the year!

The true test of the magical attraction of Raley Field occurred Saturday, July 15th. During a mega-weekend for Sacramento sports, the River Cats had to compete with four other local-regional major sporting events for fan attendance. The summer Olympic Trials enticed 23,450 to California State University. The A's–Giants Bay Bridge battle attracted 40,930 to Pac Bell Park. The Sacramento Monarchs WNBA team drew 8,348 at ARCO Arena, and the Sacramento Capitals World Team Tennis opener gathered 1,923 spectators at Gold River Stadium.

As a result, the 74,651 fans that attended those four events were not on hand to see the Fresno Grizzlies face the River Cats at Raley Field. Remarkably, yet not surprisingly, a full house of 14,111 poured into Raley Field, marking the team's 10th sell-out of the year. It was a strong and dramatic testimony to the conviction of community support, and to the hypnotic attraction of River Cats baseball played at magical Raley Field.

The Ebb and Flow of Raley Field

At each game, as the right field gate opens and the crowd begins pouring in, fans form a current of sorts, running uphill into the shade of the concourse. There, in a thick, continuous stream, the current stays to the right, nearest the field, and surges fans toward their seats, fueled by more ticket holders pouring in behind them and into the flow. The river of people pouring in from right field joins a lesser current—fed by fans entering the main gate—to cause an eddy at the confluence of the two streams—and divert fans off to other tributaries—snacks, restrooms and souvenirs.

In the third inning, another phenomenon begins: the ebb and flow of fans moving from their seats to the concourse and back. Watched from the berm, the tidal flow at Raley Field follows a predictable pattern: with two outs in the bottom of any inning, fans begin to flow up from their seats to the comfort of the concourse and as the third out is called, the flow dramatically surges. Then, as the top of the next inning begins, the tide quickly flows back into the stadium, re-filling the seats, only to be repeated five outs later.

> **RIVER CATS TRIVIA:**
> Over 60%
> (more than a half-million)
> of Raley Field's guests enter through
> the right field gate.

All Seats Are Not Created Equal

by Jeff Caraska

Before visiting the home of the Sacramento River Cats, take some time to figure out which seats will meet your highly discriminating spectating needs.

Do some scouting before you head to the ballpark. Get the best possible seats. Why settle for a grassy seat on the left field berm when you can, with a little planning, settle in down the third base line, the setting sun comfortably at your back?

Section 112, Row 29, Seat 12, $14

Prime real estate, right behind home plate. Leave the sun block at home because you're in the shade the whole time. You've got views into both dugouts (be the first in your row to spot a rhubarb brewing) and of the now-famous skyline. There's a slight blind spot deep in the left field corner, but don't fret: Jeff Walker has the same disadvantage.

Section 110, Row 15, Seat 7, $14

The Tower Bridge frames your park view on the right. If the action slows down, you can check out the action in the River Cats Dugout. Tremendous sightlines from here. This section is just to the right of home plate, so you're not far from the batter's box. If there's a play at the plate, you could end up spitting dirt.

Section 120, Row 27, Seat 11, $11

This provides an interesting view of the field as you look across from third to first. Great view of right-handed pitcher holding a runner at first. For balls hit deep down the left field line, listen to the crowd because it's out of sight. Sunset might bring a sharp reflection off some downtown Sacramento buildings. A great view for $11.

The Party Suite, $2,200

Down the left field line and high above the other paying customers, this single-game luxury suite can hold fifty fans but costs in the area of $2,000. It's decked out with plush leather armchairs and couches, a wet bar and carpeting. There are also 25 outdoor seats. Additionally, the cost includes a dozen box seats for those purists who can't stand all this decadence.

Section 205, Row 4, Seat 9

This is the Solon Club, the only upper-deck traditional stadium seating in the place. It's invitation only, but you can dream. Amenities are super. A major league view. The price you pay is staring into the sun until 8:15 or so. Unobstructed views are definitely the rule here. If you get tired of sitting, the Solon Club has a patio you can enjoy.

Section 122, Row 8, Seat 13, $8

You're directly below the Party Suite, but it costs about $2,200 less, too. This is a seat that requires a great deal of attention paid to incoming foul balls. Don't be embarrassed to bring your glove. You might need it. You're not far from the field, but well beyond third base.

Section 124, Row 20, Seat 15, $6

A panoramic view of the skyline from this seat some 200 feet from home down the left field line. You might be glad you brought your glove. This seat costs just $6 and is a short walk from a hot dog and beer stand. Who needs valet service with this kind of convenience?

The Best Seat in the House

Last winter, as the caterpillars piled and engineers graded the seating bowl in this jewel of a ballpark, any visitor could tell as they peered across the imaginary field, that fans would be right on top of the action.

"Not a bad seat in the house" rang a common refrain among fans on the concourse at an open house a few days before Opening Day. That night many season ticket holders checked out their spots in person for the first time and came away convinced that they held the best seats.

Dave Kelley, the first fan to purchase season tickets, sits in the front row, behind the plate, next to the tunnel. "The best seat in the house," claims Kelley. Randy Paragary, famed local restaurateur, watches from the home-plate-side corner of the visitors' dugout. "I thought these were the best seats in the ballpark," Paragary says. Miles Treaster, businessman and longtime Sacramento baseball supporter prefers his suite. "The suite's the only way to go," Treaster explains, standing on the open-air "balcony" of his game nest. "Indoor accommodations, as well as outdoor seats and an upper-deck view of the game." Fred Williams and his family prefer the berm. "I've sat all over this park," expresses Williams," and there's nothing like the lawn. I can spread out, lay back and the whole game unfolds in front of me."

They are all justified: each fan can lay claim that in this jewel-box of a ball yard, they have the best of the best. But, sorry, the "Best Seat in the House" is found on the center slab of the three-level patio down the left field line, about halfway between third base and the foul pole. There exists a magical spot in a magical ballpark, where two sections of guard railing meet at a

right angle, creating space for a round, umbrella-covered picnic table. It's a space with just the right elevation, just the right angle to the field, and after nightfall, the sublime view of the beautifully illuminated Tower Bridge and the "East" Sacramento skyline across the river. That table is the "Best Seat in the House." And it's "Ray's Corner."

Anyone can sit there, try it: pay five bucks for a lawn ticket and rush right out there–but you're guaranteed to find Ray Reyes already in attendance–every night. West Sacramentan Reyes, wife Emily, sister and brother-in-law, Angie and Manuel Bustillos, and sister, Esther Macias, discovered the corner at the open house and made it a point to arrive early–very early–for every game, to insure they got "the table." And there they were, every night–Ray Reyes and his group, at the "Best Seat in the House"–so it was dubbed "Ray's (or Reyes') Corner."

"We've got season tickets right down near the plate," Reyes admits with a shrug and a smile, "but we rarely sit there."

"Why would we?" Emily chimes in, "This is the best seat in the house."

Lawn Patrol

by Jeff Caraska

For the price of a matinee movie ticket, you can take in a game at Raley Field. All you need is a blanket and some shades.

The group filling the grassy berm beyond the right field fence this pleasant evening is a varied one: moms and dads trying to keep their children's energy levels under control; couples without a care in the world; teenagers, seniors and everything else in between.

If you didn't know better, you'd swear this was an assembly of people waiting for a Fourth of July fireworks display.

But the only fireworks on display this night will be provided by the hitters from the Sacramento River Cats and visiting Fresno Grizzlies.

Raley Field, now experiencing just the third homestand of its short life as a minor league ballpark, isn't the only field with festival seating where outfield bleachers might rest.

Fans of the San Bernardino Stampede of the California League enjoy this experience, as do those of the Pacific Coast League's Tucson Sidewinders and Oklahoma Redhawks.

Here at Raley Field, $5 and a fan-supplied blanket (or even better, one of those self-supporting back rests) will afford an inexpensive yet quite connected ballpark experience.

"We wanted to make sure we reached out to families," River Cats general manager Gary Arthur said. "The berm is doing exactly what it's supposed to do. It's the affordable breathing space we were looking for."

Arthur said the outfield seating is essentially a throwback. "It's like going back to the game's roots," he said. "When you'd go to a sandlot game, there usually weren't seats, so you brought a blanket to sit on and you watched a ballgame."

There are two seating berms at Raley Field. The main one stretches from dead center field to the right-field foul pole and beyond, inching its way down the right-field line toward first base. There's a smaller berm in left field.

The majority of the grass seating area offers a view into both bullpens. Souvenirs? Anyone paying more than $5 to get into this park has no chance to catch a home run ball.

On this night, a home run found its way over the center-field fence. Unfortunately for the River Cats, it was sent there by a Fresno batter. Despite pleas to toss the offending baseball back (a tradition begun in Chicago's Wrigley Field), the fan kept it, enduring the boos and catcalls from fellow lawn patrollers.

For families with children, the berm is a great alternative to the more conventional seats.

"The berm seating tickets were all that were left when we came," Tina Boccadoro of El Dorado Hills said. She brought a pair of 9-year-olds and a 6-year-old to this game. They spread out their blanket just beyond the foul pole in left.

Even though the dramatic skyline and Tower Bridge sit mostly ignored behind them, Boccadoro's group and the rest who opted for this grassy vantage point enjoyed a pretty fair sunset.

"This is really nice because it's not so confining," Boccadoro said. "The view from here is fine. We'll probably come back and get tickets for this area again."

Elsewhere on the berm, Art Nava of Orangevale and his wife are taking in the game with their 3-year-old granddaughter.

"You've got the bullpens right in front of you," he said. "It's awesome. And for $5? This was our first trip here and it won't be our last."

There's a children's play area nearby, featuring a large, inflatable trampoline. There are a couple of concessions stands close at hand as well.

When the barbecue plaza opens, customers will be seated at picnic tables in back of the berm. If the aroma resembles those tri-tip promotions put on by Raley Field's grocery store cousins, lawn patrollers will benefit from that too.

Lawn chairs aren't allowed out here. The Raley Field staff didn't want anyone's views obstructed by a fan sitting taller than a neighbor.

The sun sets behind the seats along the third baseline, so a hat and a pair of shades are probably a good idea. Oh, those cooling Delta breezes? Fans on the berm will be the first to enjoy them. For just $5.

Hundreds of River Cats' fans enjoy another cozy evening on the green.

A great view from the Solon Club deck demonstrates the popularity of the right field berm.

River Cats fans rarely had their backs to the wall in 2000.

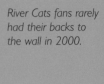

Five bucks...what a deal!

First Kids' Day packs them in on the berm.

Berm bathers soaked up the sun (in right field) all season.

West Side Story

by Will James

On Monday, May 15, 2000, at 7:51 pm PST, the curtain was raised at newly constructed Raley Field, making official the return of minor league baseball to Sacramento for the first time in 25 years. It didn't matter to the 14,111 fans in attendance at the long awaited home opener of the Oakland A's newly relocated Triple-A franchise on the west side of the Sacramento River, that frigid temperature, swirling wind, and driving rainfall were blanketing the grand event.

A few months later, after departing an Old Sacramento eatery (Rio City Café) on Front Street during one hot August evening, a strapping young man with his girlfriend stopped me and asked, "Can you direct us to where the fun and excitement is around here?" I felt compelled to borrow my response from Horace Greeley. "Of course," I replied, "I'd be happy to." And pointing toward the Tower Bridge and the Raley Field light standards above the tree line I uttered with total conviction, "Go west, young man; just follow the crowd."

This "*West Side Story*" is no musical; it is strictly of the action/adventure genre with a pinch of spicy variety sprinkled in for good measure. It's not fantasy and it's not fiction; it's just a rare experience of reality at its absolute best. So simply real in fact, the entire Raley Field/Sacramento River Cats experience oftentimes seems surreal. The new team, the new ball park, and the marvelous staff have resurrected old-time courtesy and hospitality at their highest levels. In doing so, they created a safe haven and happy playground for people of all ages to gather for a variety of reasons; all of them based on a wonderful prospect—a guaranteed payoff of pure pleasure.

No Hollywood script writer could have originated an *untrue* storyline for a baseball film that could match the unlikely but factual and fascinating creation, development, and ultimately magnificent presentation that has evolved at Raley Field with the River Cats. Not with the help of C.B. DeMille's perennial cast of thousands, nor James Cameron's grandiose full-scale staging could Hollywood fully capture the magical Raley Field/River Cats experience. Not with the intervention of Hollywood's most formidable Hall of Fame baseball characters Elmer the Great, Joe Hardy, Roy Hobbs, Crash Davis, the "Wild Thing," or Billy Chapel, could Tinsel Town match the addictive, hypnotic doses of excitement and drama that are generated from every River Cats game at Raley Field. Not even the presence of digitized heavenly powers and angels zooming around the outfield, or any other dazzling special effects, could Hollywood surpass the spectacle at this field of reality to assure that *they will come* to a small triangular-shaped parcel of land in West Sacramento.

I'm sure that the young man and his girlfriend marveled at the exquisite taste from sampling two luscious and succulent slices of our national pastime at Raley Field. Yes, indeed, this is one baseball story that need not rely on make-believe to present bigger than life impact to fans of all ages. It is the ongoing saga of '*West Side Story*'; drawing rave reviews in Y2K and scheduled for an enticing encore engagement beginning in the spring of 2001.

Wind Up

by Viola Weinberg

The pitcher stood like an angle iron—
Bent forward, legs spread, fist in mitt, squinting
Cap low against the afternoon sun.
He scuffed the mound with his feet.
Puffs of dust rose like wings on his heels.
Turning in a sly half-revolution
He checked the barbarian on first,
And forced him back, back to the bag
Like a wayward ram against the crook.

The pitch, like a poem, took time to make,
Years of wild throws from a small hand,
Decades of watching the sky or the far horizon.
It was made of everything: of his mother's laugh,
And his father's touch, transmitted through the ball
Thrown against the early summer evening stars
That hung on the blushing hem of night
With the frogs croaking their nocturnal serenade
Until the darkness covered his arm and he went in.

Then, it was finally time to come even
With the batter, who was younger and faster,
And leaner and much more hungry
For the mouth and lungs of the crowd.
The two stood against each other
And bared their teeth, their arms twitching.
Already, the pitcher had delivered chin music
And a backdoor slider that fooled the catcher.
It was time to throw his whole life across the plate.

He lifted his leg, and drew the ball against his chest,
And sent it home from the hill with an angry snap.
It came in a great tornado wheel, a Tibetan prayer wheel,
A crackling circular barn-burner
With deadly white, quiet weather at the eye of the eddy
And spirals of leather and stitch that came round and round.
Suddenly released from fingers slippery with spit
The little knot of burning hide flew across the wheelhouse
In a corkscrew curl from a sidearm, hot
As the devil's dangerous breath on the dish.

"Raley Field is all baseball aspires to be."
Brian Thornton, 32, Sacramento, all games

"This is the best thing to ever happen to Sacramento."
Jerry Oliver, 61, of Sacramento;
66 games

"A real rip-roaring realm for the River Cats to romp."
Sharon Brookshire, 39, of Grass Valley;
14 games

"Worth the wait—beautiful—thank you for the wonderful memories."
Brenda Baker, 50, of Sacramento;
61 games

"Family entertainment creating lifetime memories."
Dan Vistica, 52, Sacramento,
all games

"Great town, super team, awesome stadium! Best fans in California!"
Diana Zentner, 50, of Esparto; 30 games

"Raley Field reflects the warmth and energy of Sacramento."
Jennifer Boschkon, 10 (assisted by Steve, 34), of Davis; 12 games

"This is better than going to Oakland."
Janis Potter, 47, of West Sacramento; 4 games

"A great place for family bonding and exciting, wholesome entertainment!"
Pam Cotham, 48, of Folsom; 14 games

"Raley Field: Another gold nugget nestled on our riverbank."
Cherry Lee, 45, of Sacramento

"Intimate."
Dennis Lordan, 40, of Walnut Creek; 1 game

"Intense fun, outstanding architecture, a place to be proud of."
Debra Gregory, 46, of West Sacramento, 40 games

"Raley Field is a beautiful flower in a blighted garden."
Kenneth Kimble, 76, of Davis; 30+ games

"Big, Bold, Bodacious and Beautiful."
Buzz Young, 52, of Vacaville

"Beautiful setting – great baseball. Thanks for an exciting season."
Chris Powell, 68, of Sacramento; 4 games

"It's Music Circus without the tent."
Paul Bossenmeier, Attorney

"We laid 3.18 miles of syrup lines to 7 stands and 28 units."
Kirk Lopez, Coca-Cola

"Everything is 1st Class here! It's nice to see players on the fringe of the majors."
Don Mashburn, Hiram Johnson softball coach

"Raley Field is fun and has something for everyone."
Bill Sifers, 47, of Sacramento; 8 games

"I love baseball, I love being at the ballpark, I just love Raley Field."
Dave Hillver, Rocket Scientist and food vendor

"In 17 years as a concessionaire I've worked Super Bowls, World Series' and NBA Finals and the fans at Raley Field are by far the friendliest and tip the best."
Reginald Barnett, "Mr Peanut Tosser"

"It gives me a major league feeling in a fabulous little park. It's terrific."
Mark Tibke, Roofer

"What a great place to see a ballgame. There's not a bad seat in the house. This is a wonderful success for everyone."
Tom Murphy, Banker

"Great fun! Friendly... clean... safe... excellent food... and DINGER!"
Diane Smith, 52, of Sacramento, 10 games

"We love it! Spring training all summer long!"
Bill and Thelma Bess, (60, 62), of Lotus; 15, 20 games

"A family oriented park staffed by professional and courteous people."
Annette Shaw, 40, of West Sacramento; 47 games

"Above and beyond AAA ballparks —— major league all the way."
Marilyn Abbott, 57, of West Sacramento; 25 games

"Raley Field is the Eighth Wonder of the World and a dream come true."–*Number One Fan, Dave Kelley*

Like Father, Like Son

by Doug Curley

"Dad, does Harvard have a baseball team?"
"What's the name of their team?"
"Are they a very good team?"
"What California colleges have a good baseball team?"
"And what are their names?"
"Should I go to a two-year or four-year college before I turn pro?"
"How can I make sure I get on a team near you and Mom, and Claire?"

Thanks to the arrival of the Sacramento River Cats, those are the types of questions I constantly field from my 8-year-old son, Patrick. Don't get me wrong, I love the fact that I finally have a child (I'm now closer to 50 than 35) that has become a sports fan. It just gets a little embarrassing when Dad doesn't have all the answers.

My love for sports came about when I saw my first World Series game on a color television. It was my Stepdad's beloved Dodgers (he grew up on the East Coast rooting for the Brooklyn Dodgers and the Boston Red Sox) vs. the Minnesota Twins. If my memory serves me correct, the Dodgers were down two games to none. Claude Osteen was on the mound for the L.A. Blue, after big guns Sandy Koufax and Don Drysdale had been beaten in the first two games in Minnesota. I don't remember the score, but it was a classic, low scoring pitching duel. The Dodgers won. I was hooked.

From that time on I watched games every week, kept scrapbooks on several big league sports, played the games, memorized stats. To this day the first thing I do every morning is spend about 20 minutes with the local sports page. But what has changed now is that I'm greeted every morning with the question: "How did the River Cats do last night?"

Now before the River Cats arrived in town, Patrick had had some exposure to baseball. He's been playing organized ball since he was four. He and I and the rest of the family closely followed the Mark McGwire/ Sammy Sosa home run chase with history. He even attended a Giants-Mariners game during the first year of interleague play. But baseball, like most sports, was really something he did to amuse his father. It also was an opportunity to purchase cotton candy and add to his collection of memorabilia—logo balls, pennants, posters and bobble-head dolls.

The game matters now. The players have names and positions. The rules of the game are important. And the process by which one becomes a professional baseball player is of utmost interest. This overnight change in attitude is perhaps due to a combination of a growing appreciation of the game through participation (he has now completed a second year of hitting the ball pitched by a pitching machine rather than the lowly batting-tee) along with an increasing awareness that cotton candy really is pretty gross.

Whatever the reason, my son became a true baseball fan following the third inning of the first River Cats game he attended. With the Cats down 2-0, and the first round of hot dogs, drinks and nachos consumed, Patrick's Mom asked if he was ready to go search for a logo ball at the gift shop. His response: "Not until the game's over Mom."

Mary Androvich digs into a dog while watching the Cats.

Bill Neuffer and daughter with her souvenir baseball.

River Cats garb fit the bill for this youngster at Raley Field.

Brandi DeGeorge at Kids' Day.

Outside-in view of Mike Bell with (left to right) Rusty Ramirez, Dalton Bell, Cienna Bell

Players signed hats and balls tossed from kids on the berm.

Kids Photo Gallery

"All in the family" at the ballgame.

Cool twins on a hot day at Raley Field.

Jason Cable gives daughter a boost.

River Cats exec. VP, Warren Smith, and son Dominic.

Not every fan was overcome by the magic of Raley Field.

Autograph hound, on the prowl for future Oakland A's.

Paul Bossenmeier, local sports official, cries "Kill the ump!"

Fans Photo Gallery

Kristy McAuliffe and Mike Eady are ready!

Randy and Laurie Miller, loyal fans out for game two.

Is Kathi Brown proud of her foul ball or what?

"Sportraits" artist Jolene Jessie cheered from Section 107.

George Christopolus (right), Son Theo and cousins.

Former Solons players Cuno Barragan and Ritchie Myers.

Former Solons players Gus Stathos and Art Anacich.

Ricci Dula and Mom, Paula.

Ed Sarmento and his buddies tour the concourse.

Jerry and Bill Oliver attended nearly every game.

Danielle, Randy and Janet Wagner on a beautiful night at the game.

The Scoggins family had a great time on the berm.

Home Opener in Oakland! Richard Reynolds and his party.

Terry Rasmussen and son, Eric, frosh QB at San Diego Univ.

Joe Androvich "liked Raley Field more than Pac Bell Park."

Sailor Jack, Bingo and Angela Tanghetti.

Bob and Ruth Worthen with their girls, Madie and Candace and Mary Androvich (l).

Gary and Phyllis Ordway in the ballpark he helped construct.

Ron Caceres and daughter, Nicole, sit behind the visitors' dugout.

Arthur Vigner, celebrates the 4th at the ball game.

Don Mashburn, Hiram Johnson H.S. softball coach, a regular.

Michael and Libby Parr, behind home plate.

Al Manfredi (center) and family in deep right-center field.

Ray Webber and family in the shade of Section 119.

Kathy, Sarah, Meghan and Pat Butler actually keep score!

Sharon Sammons, Rudy Castro and Toni Steelman stop in the current as fans pour in.

Izzy Smith and Cy Opper, "The French Fry Kids."

Tammy Newbert and her friends were first at Raley Field to arrive in River Cat ears.

Chris Holman, Brian Ducy, Michael Holman and Tyler Steele waiting to see Raley Field.

Harry Devine in his 50s vintage Solons jacket.

Pat Wanta and Terry Plushanski share a laugh in left field.

Mark Marvelli, Bob Androvich and Brett Marshall walked over from Old Sacramento.

Julie Madison (Josue Espada's girlfriend) and Stephanie Larkin (Roberto Vaz's fiance).

800,000th fan, John Cope, wife Sandy, daughter Samantha, and grandson, Trey Edwards.

Jim Anderson strikes a familiar pose behind the plate.

Timothy Busfield with kids on Opening Night.

Former Solons players Bud Watkins (L) Cuno Barragan and Richie Myers enjoy a night out at Raley Field.

Raley Field works its magic on a happy couple.

Cal Bear fans have room in their hearts for the Cats.

Jim Stephens, CBS High School boys basketball coach.

Golf professional Jim Salazar takes a rare day off to visit Raley Field.

Raley Field brought out the smiles in everyone.

Alicia Gonzalez shows off the new program.

Stacy and Randy Paragary get away from the restaurant.

Ted Olson, watching from the berm at a rare day game.

Chuck and Frances Collings, the River Cats' #1 fans.

Mark Tibke could not get over the view of "East" Sacramento.

Emily Reyes proudly displays her autographed ball.

Vera Solorio enjoys a game with son, Andre.

Dean Halstead and pal on the upper concourse.

Former balllplayer Lavelle Freeman & Bill Yurtin laugh it up.

Mr. amd Mrs. Gary Roberts on a warm summer evening.

Jazz ambassador Joyce Diamond after her original rendition of the national anthem.

Gary and Jim Meade, armed with mitts, ready for the stray foul ball.

Bob and Roberta Rakela have been baseball fans for many years in Sacramento.

Geri Shumaker and Bryan and Beverly Mier had a sensational time goofing off at Raley Field.

The right field berm brought out the kid in many a Raley Field fan.

Ray Reynoso gives Raley Field a big "thumbs-up!"

Legendary Cordova Cat, Guy Anderson, and wife, Karen.

Howard and Nancy Taylor on their way out of the park.

Sean Smith, celebrating part of his bachelor party at magical Raley field.

Adam, Bob and Emily Hall enjoy Opening Night.

Dawn and Jack Cornelius sat in both suites and seats..

Former Texas leaguer Don Murphy caught mid-dog..

John Moist, president of local SABR chapter.

Three generations of baseball fans from the Spooner family.

Brett Marshall, ready to sample a Dinger Dog.

Greg Abbott and Rebecca Malakian in Oakland.

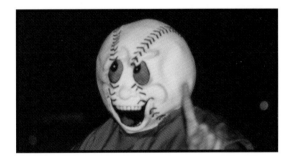

This guy was kind of "into it..."

Local athletic supporters Miles Treaster and John Stafford.

Bill Curren of Moxie, samples the ballpark fare.

Tom, Whitney and Sheila Grouvhog.

Mike Hoss and his son, Andrew, sat in Section 108.

Michael James and Michael, Jr. hold first Raley Field homer.

Jerome and Tink Rolf have always been baseball fans.

Stands so white, his elbows folded like wet tissue

Cheeks flaring scarlet in the blistering heat
A gawky monument high atop the 18" mound
A seven-foot beast from the Pacific Northwest

Stands like a derrick in Arabia, dunes shifting
His cold eyes pierce the little Dominican batter
With spare, mechanical flickers and naked
Nineteen year-old jitters on bony knuckles

by Viola Weinberg

The Next Big One from Tacoma

Down on the plate, the batter looks terrified
The head of the bat drawn almost to his cheek
A tick visible from the bleachers, desperately
Brave little man bares his teeth and waves his rear

Aw, come on El Grande, you want me

The Next Big One from Tacoma bursts
Into the pitch, windmill and mitt and blade
It tears through the heavy air, born to rip

The guns behind the plate rear up and
The scouts clock the slingshot—96 and flying
But it falls out of its screw, out of the trajectory
Out of Big One's control and into little zurdo's zone

Wham! The Next Big One looks up

As the ball arcs over his high head, up over
His astonished eyes with their fluttering lids
Up! And, O Mio Dio, over the fence, he groans

The little batter, now a great hitter, runs the bases
His mother in the D.R. kneels in the church with her
Hands knotted in prayer, feels sudden light and righteousness
Just three cantos in, the jubilation tremolo like a weeping fan.

THE NEXT BIG ONE FROM TACOMA

"Raley Field is what childhood memories are made of."
The Wishek Family of Elk Grove; 20+ games

"Thank you, Mr. Raley."
Lis Lentsch, 46, of Citrus Heights;
7 games

**"Great games!–Less Filling!–
Go Cats Go!"**
Barry Kalar, 53, of West Sacramento;
60+ games

"Raley Field is the cat's meow!"
Charmaine Doyle, 47, of Elk Grove;
30 games

"Grassy, classy, green as a bean."
Buzz Jones, 52, of Vacaville

**"Everything that's great about
Sacramento: people, atmosphere,
weather and baseball!"**
Bob Gutierrez, 47, of Diamond Springs;
6 games

"Cats Came–Cats Saw–Cats Conquered!"
John Palmerini, 64, of Sacramento; 6 games

**"A mass of humanity / Cheering on the boys / A bountiful bowl /
Full of happy noise!"**
Hal Heath, 39, of Fair Oaks; "almost all" games

"Baseball–Crackerjacks–Peanuts–and River Cats!"
Kristene Marshall, 37, of Sacramento; 7 games

"This is my new house of worship!"
Michael Parsons, 42, of Auburn; 20 games

"Best thing to happen to Sacramento in my lifetime!"
John "Corkey" Colbert, 53, of West Sacramento; 40 games

"Spectacular scenery, friendly people, great weather and a good time!"
Judy Broshar, 49, of Sacramento; 20 games

**"The best field to watch the very first baseball game! (P.S. We don't have
baseball in Iceland.)"**
Ms. Ragnhildur Sverrisdottir, 40, now of Davis; her first baseball game ever

"Lookin' Good / Standin' Tall / Come On Cats / Let's Play Ball!"
Mrs. R. Flatt, 54, of El Dorado Hills; 6 games

"Baseball is a religion–Raley Field is a cathedral."
Vince Doyle, 41, of Elk Grove; 45 games

"Recapturing a part of youth–nine innings at a time."
Cliff Hoffman, 42, of Mather; 42 games

"Time with my son at Raley Field watching the River Cats? —— Priceless!"
Gary and Hunter Lunsford, 34 and 2 and a half

**"Riveting; Inviting; Victorious; Energetic; Rewarding; Cat Fever; Addicting;
Terrific; Sensational!"**
Linda Pyle and Tim Rice, 49 and 56, of West Sacramento; 67 games

"Pinch yourself to see if you are dreaming!"
Rick Morales, 43, of Orangevale; 6 games

"Fun, fun, fun, and more fun!"

Larry Freeman, 51, of Orangevale;
30 games

"Great for families. Great for friends. Great for fans—Thanks!"
Richard Germoles, 70, of Sacramento; 8 games

"Raley Field is family time."
Manuel Guido, 48, of Sacramento; 55 games

"I've been to three games—and wait for more."
Clark Ireland, 33, of Sacramento; 3 games

"The beautiful fruit of labor of many dedicated people."
Gary Ordway, 59, of Foresthill; 32 games

"Green grass, blue sky, strikes, balls, it's summer in Sacramento."
Richard Glovin, 46, of Sacramento; 4 games

"A special green carpet for summertime fun – it's the best!"
Curt Kaufman, 50, of Sacramento; 15 games

"The best little baseball field west of the river."
Joe Alameida, 51, of Roseville; 10 games

"A true 'field of dreams' for Sacramento and West Sacramento."
Sue Colbert, 50, of West Sacramento; 40 games

"Sacramento and Baseball – a marriage made in heaven."
Jackie Laca, 45, of Sacramento; 21 games

"Raley Field single-handedly changed the face of Sacramento."
Bob Van Noy, 50, of Sacramento; 4 games

"Always a good experience! Great fun! It made my summer!"
Heather Smith, 22, of Sacramento; 19 games

"The stadium's fantastic—players the best, and the fans magnificent."
Claudia Stowe, 50, of El Dorado; 67 games

"You built it, the fans came!"
Tony Beard, Jr., 50, of Carmichael; 70 games

"Picturesque center field view portrays essence of players striving for perfection."
Bernice Bettencourt and Jane Braby of Napa, attended 2 games

*"Sacramento and Baseball—
a marriage made in Heaven."*
Jackie Laca, 45, of Sacramento;
21 games

Mitt on a Stick

Following the untimely rainfall on opening day in mid-May, harsh weather passed and fair weather prevailed in the Sacramento Valley. With the arrival of clear and sunny skies, abundant, bright sunshine regularly glazed Raley Field.

It was quite apparent that some River Cats fans would have to contend with a relentless, broad beam of sunlight that day after day took its natural, predictable, gradual time to slip below the stadium roof on the third base side of the ballpark.

As the sun drooped to a horizontal bearing, all the fans from first base out, along the right field line were in the "sun zone." These fans would need something special to deal with Mother Nature's golden, glaring beams. Some used baseball gloves they brought with them to the game, but as the sun lingered, the weight of a glove caused many an arm to fall.

Will James, of Circus Catch Publishing, suggested a solution: Mitt On a Stick—a printed image of a mitt affixed to a forearm-long stick that would allow the fan to sit back and relax in their seat and shade their eyes from the sun without the fatigue extending their arm for three or four innings.

"'Mitt on a Stick' territory," James said, walking from the right field gate and up to the concourse minutes before the start of a contest. Hundreds of fans were angled toward home plate, their own personal style and versatility in play in various "mitt-on-a-stick" postures.

"There are four basic 'mitt-on-a-stick' positions," James explained. The most common is the

Left handed 'Military Salute' position.

Double "Peek-a-Boo."

Southpaw "Peek-a-Boo" style.

"Reversible/Switch Handed"

The consumnate "Scout" position.

"Reversible/Switch Handed" position, using either the left or right hand. "This position requires the fan to extend the arm toward the sun, to obscure it whether or not it is in direct line with home plate." Options of using either arm, and a backhand or forehand (to the sun) block, make it the most popular.

Many fans prefer the "Military Salute." This option is especially effective when the sun is well above the field but still a nuisance. The index finger is brought to the extreme right side of the forehead above the temple and placed at a diagonal angle with the thumb tucked in tight to the upper cheekbone.

"'The Scout' position is more compact," James asserts. The hand is kept parallel to the ground and tucked in tight to the face with the thumb curled along the temple, providing a sunroof extending from the top of the forehead which minimizes arm weariness.

The final option is "The Peek-a-Boo," and is assumed only out of absolute desperation when the sun is just slightly above the roof and in a virtual direct line with home plate and your line of vision. It's the least effective option because blocking the sun means blocking the view of the game, but it's not out of the question for some members of the "mitt on a stick" section.

How about a mitt on a stick?

Left hands and sunglasses.

My Amazing Baseball Career

by Ed Goldman

Since the Dodgers left New York City for Southern California about a year before I did, I've always felt a special affinity for the team. I've thought of its members as trailblazers for my family: if they could leave behind the excitement, color, summer-long humidity, winter-long garbage collectors' strike and soaring domestic crime rate of Gotham for the year-round sunshine, emphysema and post-dinner inactivity of Los Angeles, why, so could we.

Not that I had much choice in the matter. I was not quite 8 years old at the time. My father had retired, at the age of 42, from the New York City Fire Department, and saw the West Coast as everything Manhattan wasn't–which is to say, inhabitable. New York was a great place to live if you either had a lot of money or a lot of passion–for art, culture, crowds, domestic crime and so forth. But if your daily view of it was dominated by burning apartment houses, screaming victims and traffic challenges (my dad drove the front of one of those unwieldy hook-and-ladder firetrucks), the city's glamour was a little harder to detect.

So we ended up in a suburb of Southern California called Lakewood and within a year or so, I was playing park league baseball. I had to. If you came to California from New York, you had to play baseball even if, like me, you really couldn't play baseball. This was because my parents no longer found it acceptable nor understandable that I could enjoy sitting at the desk in my room, writing and drawing, for hours on end. "Get some fresh air!" was the command–though, given the fact that our new home was where the phenomenon known as the "smog alert" originated, this might have been shouted more ironically than I was old enough to appreciate.

The point was if you lived in a place where the sun shone 90 percent of the time–even if it did so with enough toxins to turn your lungs to a substance not unlike papier maché–then, by God, you were going to get yourself outside and enjoy every lousy minute of it.

So I played baseball, or at least played at it. It got me outside and it didn't seem too taxing: the gag that baseball was "two-and-a-half minutes of action crammed into two-and-a-half hours" was already making the rounds, and for a kid whose athletic prowess had yet to materialize (I'm still waiting), that sounded just about right.

But there was a problem. In addition to being almost clinically uncoordinated, I was nearsighted, though it wouldn't be verified until I was 12 years old and got fitted for my first pair of mainframes. (I would be disappointed to learn that the fuzzy dots I always saw in the distance were not, as I theorized, atoms; they were just whatever the hell happened to be in the distance: cars, buildings, trees, relatives).

As a result, I was equally unreliable as a hitter or fielder. When left-handed batters stepped up, I was shifted to right field (while the first and second basemen drew much closer together). For right-handed batters, I played deep left (and the shortstop played what could have been called shallow left). I didn't blame anyone. In all fairness, with my eyesight and agility I was as likely to get beaned by a bouncing ground ball as a line drive–and was, repeatedly, including at bat (I had a tendency to lean over to get a better look at objects heading my way).

The coach–a pretty nice man except for the fact that he continually reminded his son, one of my teammates, that he was a thundering disappointment to him every single minute of his life–told me he admired my pluck. I assumed that "pluck" was the sound the baseball made each time it struck my skull; I thanked him, but didn't want him to get his hopes up that this was a skill I'd be refining as the season went on.

A.J. Hinch gives new meaning to the term "Inside-out swing!"

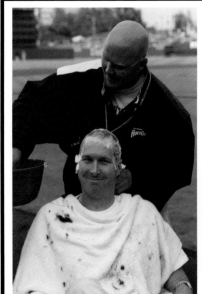

Tom Glick and Warren Smith are shorn of their locks after losing a pre-season bet that season-long attendance would not exceed 750, 000.

I guess the major-league insult of my exceedingly minor-league career came when I arrived at one of our dinner-hour games and discovered that another boy, approximately my own size and coloring, was sitting on the

This is the Big Apple around here!

Game on!

bench wearing a shirt that had my own number on it. He was a ringer—or, more precisely, a stunt boy. The coach had recruited him from a nearby Catholic school in the hope of adjusting the team's 0-17 win-loss record.

"Now, Edward," the coach said, using my formal name in the time-honored tradition of coaches talking to weenies, "you have to understand that the city's park league doesn't allow us to substitute players. So we're not really doing that this evening. Instead, a boy who'll be called Edward Goldman, who looks like the real Edward Goldman, is going to play for the first, oh, seven or eight innings. Now please change into this other t-shirt behind the backstop and pull this cap over your eyes."

I'm proud to say that my stunt boy played a valiant game— and would have gotten away with the masquerade were it not for his insistence on issuing Hail Marys in the batter's box and crossing himself after making particularly good catches. These were not the things a boy named Goldman would have been likely to do, and the ruse was exposed in the bottom of the fifth inning.

"Well, Edward, you can go into the game now," the coach came over to the bench to tell me. A moment later, he came back and asked why I was still sitting there.

"I have one more Hail Mary to go," I said.

The River Cats' Premiere Season

As if the return of Triple-A baseball to magnificent Raley Field wasn't enough, the River Cats' premiere season delivered far more than any fans expected. As the team departed on the longest road trip in baseball history, the baseball buzz around town still swirled about progress at Raley Field

Opening Night, most of the crowd pouring into Raley Field was unaware that the Sacramento River Cats (Vancouver Canadians) were defending Triple-A Champions and that Adam Piatt and Barry Zito were two of the hottest players in the minor leagues. The fact that baseball was finally coming back seemed enough to excite area enthusiasts.

Soon, though, fan favorites emerged – Piatt, Zito, veteran Paul Sorrento, slugging infielders Eric Martins, Mark Bellhorn and Jose Ortiz, and outfielders Mario Encarnacion, Roberto Vaz and Bo Porter – and the team got hot. No matter what the parent club Oakland A's did to disrupt the roster, new stars emerged and the River Cats continued their dominance. Sorrento retired June 14th, replaced by another venerable vet, Steve Decker. Piatt and Zito were gone for good to the A's by July 23rd. Eric Byrnes and Justin Miller stepped up to fill their roles.

The River Cats finished the first half of the season in first place, 14 games over .500, and then finished the second half of July with a 15-3 record. All the while, the A's moved players back and forth as if they were in a rotisserie league, making over 100 active list transactions during the year. On their way to winning the Southern Division crown of the Pacific Coast League with a 90-54 mark, 56 players wore the River Cats' uniform.

Although eliminated in the first round of the playoffs, the premiere season of the Sacramento River Cats was undeniably a huge success. Jose Ortiz was named PCL Most Valuable Player and the Sacramento River Cats were named Triple-A Team of the Year by Baseball America magazine.

Here Today–Gone Tomorrow

Minor League Baseball is noted for its constant movement of talent–new, young prospects on their way up and familiar, older veterans on rehab, or on their way out of the game.

As much as fans loved the players, Sacramento was the last place any of these athletes wanted to end up: Oakland and "The Show," was just down the road. And as cool as Raley Field is, all of the players longed to play in the concrete canyon of Network Associates Coliseum 90 miles west. To make matters weirder, River Cats fans were subjected to more wheeling and dealing than any other team in Triple-A baseball. The River Cats' premiere season was highlighted by a non-stop revolving door of talent in and out of the clubhouse beyond the left-center field fence.

Fifty-six different players suited up in River Cats' pinstripes this season. Over 120 transactions were made throughout the season. Adam Piatt made three trips to the parent club, ending up with the A's for good on July 13th. Ariel Prieto made three trips up, as well. The A's plucked hurler Mark Mulder from the Sacramento roster after the big lefty had pitched just eight-and-a-third innings in a River Cats' uniform. He never threw a pitch at Raley Field. Just as Sacramento fans were falling in love with Barry Zito, off he went to the A's, never to be seen in Sactown after July 23rd.

During the year, Sacramento used 23 different starting pitchers during the course of the regular season. Zito and Jon Ratliff led the staff with 18 starts each and Marcus Jones registered 17 starting assignments. Within the span of 90 victories, 22 different pitchers were credited with at least one win.

Paul Sorrento, an 11-year major league vet, made a stop in town before hanging up the spikes for good on June 14th. Jeremy Giambi and John Jaha, Oakland sluggers, spent time on the River Cats' roster on short rehabilitation assignments. Steve Decker joined the club in late June to replace Sorrento and add some maturity and solid leadership to the young squad.

Then, at the end of the season, A.J. Hinch, Jose Ortiz, Bo Porter and Scott Service joined the A's for the run for the Western Division title and the American League Playoffs, giving River Cats fans more chances to see their favorite players in action.

Illustration: "Starting 5 and 9" by Jolene Jessie

The original five River Cats' starting pitchers and catcher (left to right): Jon Ratliff, Barry Zito, Mark Mulder, Chad Harville, Ariel Prieto and A.J. Hinch

Jose Ortiz

Jose Ortiz, 23-year-old infielder, had quite a year. Besides being named PCL MVP for 2000, being selected for the PCL All-Star Team, receiving Player-of-the-Week honors in August, capturing the River Cats' MVP "Savage Trophy," Ortiz was named by Baseball America magazine as the best second baseman AND the Minor League Player of the Year for 2000. ••• Ortiz batted .351 with 182 hits, including 34 doubles, five triples, 24 homers 108 rbi. ••• He finished the year with the Oakland A's.

Name	Pos	B/T	Ht	Wt	DOB	Birthplace	Residence
Danny Ardoin	C/1B	R/R	6-0	215	07-08-74	Mamou, LA	Villa Platt, LA
Mark Bellhorn	INF	S/R	6-4	214	08-21-74	Boston, MA	Oviedo, FL
Will Brunson	P	L/L	6-5	185	03-20-70	Irving, TX	Bulverde, TX
Terry Burrows	P	L/L	6-0	203	11-28-68	Lake Charles, LA	Lake Charles, LA
Bryan Corey	P	R/R	6-0	170	10-21-73	Thousand Oaks, CA	Phoenix, AZ
Mario Encarnacion	OF	R/R	6-2	205	09-24-77	Bani, DR	Bani, DR
Josue Espada	INF	R/R	5-10	175	08-30-75	Santurce, PR	Carolina, PR
Chad Harville	P	R/R	5-9	180	09-16-76	Selmer, TN	Savannah, TN
A.J. Hinch	C	R/R	6-1	207	05-15-74	Waverly, LA	Scottsdale, AZ
Tim Kubinski	P	L/L	6-4	205	01-20-72	Pullman, WA	Tempe, AZ
Frank Lankford	P	R/R	6-2	190	03-26-71	Atlanta, GA	Atlanta, GA
Terrence Long	OF	L/L	6-1	190	02-29-76	Montgomery, AL	Millbrook, AL
T.R. Marcinczyk	1B	R/R	6-3	195	10-11-73	Plainville, CT	Plainville, CT
Eric Martins	INF	R/R	5-9	170	11-19-72	East Los Angeles, CA	Rowland Heights, CA
Mark Mulder	P	L/L	6-6	200	08-05-77	South Holland, IL	South Holland, IL
Chris Norton	C	R/R	6-2	215	09-21-70	Greenville, MS	Longwood, FL
Jose Ortiz	INF	R/R	5-9	177	06-13-77	Santo Domingo, DR	Santo Domingo, DR
Adam Piatt	INF/OF	R/R	6-2	195	02-08-76	Chicago, IL	Fort Myers, FL
Ariel Prieto	P	R/R	6-2	247	10-22-69	Havana, Cuba	Miami, FL
Jon Ratliff	P	R/R	6-4	195	12-22-71	Syracuse, NY	Clay, NY
Rich Sauveur	P	L/L	6-4	195	11-23-63	Falls Church, VA	Bradenten, FL
Bert Snow	P	R/R	6-1	190	03-23-77	Brooksville, FL	Brooksville, FL
Roberto Vaz	OF	L/L	5-9	195	03-15-75	Brooklyn, NY	Tuscaloosa, AL
Barry Zito	P	L/L	6-4	205	05-13-78	Las Vegas, NV	Las Vegas, NV

The Longest Road Trip

by James L. Burton

On Monday, May 15th, at 2:22 in the afternoon, after 40 days, 41 nights, and 37 games, the Sacramento River Cats Inaugural Season 2000 road trip arrived at Sacramento International Airport on Alaska Airlines Flight #356. The Pacific Coast League Baseball Team, a team that had traveled to Modesto, Fresno, Tacoma, Salt Lake City, Oakland, Salt Lake City, Albuquerque, Colorado Springs, Fresno and Tacoma, had finally returned home. The road trip, the longest ever to start a professional baseball season, was history. The longest road trip was over.

Danny Ardoin, a River Cats catcher and former Huntsville (Alabama) Star, summarized the trip to sportswriter Mark McCarter of The Huntsville Times in one word: the road trip had been a "grind." Jim Van Vliet, the Sacramento Bee sportswriter who accompanied the team and returned home after 21 days, rejoined the team in Colorado Springs following the 4-game series in Albuquerque. Looking back, the 50-year-old Van Vliet said, "It was too long; way too long. I don't think I could have survived all of it. I couldn't wait for the 15th."

Hitting coach Roy White, who played 15 seasons with the New York Yankees and two seasons with Japan's Pacific Coast League Tokyo Giants, wasn't fazed: "It wasn't too bad."

The road trip, which began on April 6th in Fresno, was the second longest in Pacific Coast League history—only the Sacramento Solons 88-game journey in 1948 was longer. Unlike the Solons, who had been forced to finish the season on the road following a mid-July fire that burned Edmonds Field to the ground, the River Cats' road trip did have a silver lining. The River Cats, who had been forced to start the season on the road due to delays in the construction of Raley Field, returned home with a record of 22 wins and 15 losses. As a result of the road trip, the River Cats could look forward to playing 18 games in July and 24 games in August at Raley Field. The road trip had resulted in the mother of all home stands.

Walt Horn, the team's certified athletic trainer, was responsible for team travel and equipment. At first, Horn noted, "I didn't know if I was going to be prepared." Horn, the consummate professional, was ready: 30 players bags, four bat bags with 25-30 bats in each, a couple of extra sets of catcher's equipment, one trunk for video gear, two ball bags with 100 balls in each, a couple of extra uniform bags, extra helmets, and additional gear. Fortunately, at every city, the team would receive "more stuff" via United Parcel Service. The new supplies would make it less likely that trainer Horn would have to borrow equipment, something that Horn would prefer not to do. "I didn't have to borrow anything. That was a good feeling." Starting with 70 pieces, "one-half to two-thirds full," the problem became accumulating too much gear and "busting at the seams." The team arrived home with 80 pieces. Also, Horn added, "We didn't really lose any gear and none of the guys lost any personal gear."

Fresno-Tacoma-Salt Lake City-Oakland.

On Wednesday, April 5th, pitcher Rich Sauveur and his teammates rode the bus from West Sacramento to Modesto to play an exhibition game against the California League Modesto A's. The 36-year-old Sauveur, a veteran of 21 major and minor league teams, informed Vacaville Reporter sports page editor Tim Roe, "We're basically going to be living out of a suitcase for a month." Outfielder Roberto Vaz advised Bee sportswriter Jim Van Vliet, "My suitcases are so packed it looks like there's a body in them." And pitcher Terry Burrows told Van Vliet, "I'm throwing stuff in two suitcases. I might have to have my wife send me new stuff at each stop."

With a 12-2 win over the Class A team, the River Cats opened the Pacific Coast League season with a 10-2 loss against the Class AAA Fresno Grizzlies. Following four games in Fresno, three games in Tacoma, and four games in Salt Lake City, the team arrived in Oakland and the Holiday Inn with a record of 7-4 and a four-game "home" series against the Calgary Cannons. The flight had been delayed and the hotel rooms were not ready. Talking about the road trip with Jim Van Vliet, catcher A.J. Hinch commented: "Twelve games is considered a long road trip. That's how many we played when we got here. You start thinking. We'll make it. Then you realize there's 25 more."

Unlike several other River Cats, who had already played with the Major League Oakland A's at Network Associates Coliseum, outfielder Mario Encarnacion was happy. "I said to myself. Someday, I'm going to be here. This is very nice."

Winning two and losing two against the Florida Marlins PCL team, the River Cats returned to Salt Lake City on April 21st with a 9-6 record.

Oakland-Salt Lake City-Albuquerque-Colorado Springs-Fresno

Losing four of their first five games in Salt Lake City, the River Cats arrived in Albuquerque carrying a 10-10 record and a virus among the players that had probably been picked up in Utah. Six players and Manager Bob Geren suddenly felt really ill. Walt Horn: "The guys got sick in Albuquerque. First, it was two guys, then two more, and then two more." The 36-hour flu apparently didn't slow the team down. The River Cats won three of four to post a 13-11 record. Noting that an umpire crew who stayed on to work the next series in Salt Lake had also been hit by the virus, Horn noted, "We were lucky. We got through it."

With custom-made leather jackets presented to the players in Albuquerque "as a token of appreciation" from owner president Art Savage and general manager Gary Arthur, the team moved from April to May and from Albuquerque to Colorado Springs. After winning three of four, the 16-12 River Cats flew from Colorado Springs to Salt Lake City and back to Fresno. Winning all four games in Fresno, the 20-12 River Cats anticipated a quick, Wednesday morning, May 10th bus ride up Highway 99 to Sacramento for a half-day break. The team would then fly to Seattle for the Tacoma series. There was only one problem. The charter bus had been stolen.

Manager Bob Geren had been informed by Doubletree Hotel management early Wednesday morning that the bus had been stolen during the night. Geren couldn't believe it. No bus? The driver, according to Geren and pitching coach Rick Rodriguez, looked and sounded like comedian Cheech Marin. When the driver went to the front of the hotel, where he usually parked the bus, there was an empty space. The bus wasn't there. The driver was certain. "Oh, man, the bus was stolen." Hotel management suggested that Geren find vans and rental cars to get the team back up to Sacramento. Suddenly, the driver remembered that he had taken the older model bus to the shop on Tuesday afternoon for repair. The "oldest bus in the world" suddenly reappeared and the team was back on the road. Geren recalled, "He was a nice guy, but he must have blacked out or something."

Sacramento-Seattle-Sacramento

Walt Horn looked at the break in Sacramento as an opportunity: "It was a chance to dump stuff." On May 11th, the team flew to Seattle and bused north on Interstate 5 to Tacoma. Following a 5-2 win over Rainiers pitcher 6' 11" Ryan "Space Needle" Anderson, the end of the road trip, and a new beginning at Raley Field, was in sight. Roberto Vaz told Jim Van Vliet, "We can't wait to get there." Shortstop Jose Ortiz had only been able to talk to his 6-month-old son on the telephone. Ortiz, who had not seen his son since February when he left the Dominican Republic, told Van Vliet, "He still thinks I'm a telephone." Similarly, catcher Danny Ardoin, who missed his 2-year-old son and wife, told Van Vliet: "That's been the hardest part of the trip, not being able to see them. It's a killer."

With two wins and three losses against the Rainiers and an outstanding 22-15 record, the team departed Seattle-Tacoma International Airport on Alaska Airlines at 12:39 on Monday afternoon. The team was one hour and 43 minutes away from home. The trip was one for the record book. And, the team had played great baseball.

For season ticket holders Dan and Tess Barboza, the road trip had also been way too long. Dan Barboza: "When I bought the [season] tickets, I was really excited. And then the road trip dragged on and on and on. We wanted to see some baseball. The road trip was getting on our nerves. We started arguing. We weren't affectionate. And then, when they came home, it was so great. It was like we were on our honeymoon all over again."

Paul Sorrento winds up to bash one deep.

Players Photo Gallery

Opposing players knew they were crossing into "The Twilight Zone" at Raley Field.

Adam Piatt warms up for the first "Home Game"... in Oakland.

See ya! Eric Byrnes blasts a homer on his way to batting .333.

Fan appreciation night raffle brought team owner Art Savage together with Eric Martins.

Jose Ortiz slides home safely with one of his 107 runs scored in 2000.

For many months Barry Zito and Adam Piatt were still Canadians.

Barry Zito–Mid-March: No mound. Mid-July: Up to the A's starting rotation.

Bo Porter thrilled fans with incredible circus catches all season.

Pre-Game Ballet

Bob Geren:"Which way did they go?"

The best .266 hitter in baseball... Mark Bellhorn.

"Cool" Roberto Vaz, waiting to take the field.

All-Star 2nd baseman and PCL MVP smiled all year long.

Fiery, explosive, ever hustling Eric Byrnes.

High-fives follow another River Cats' homer.

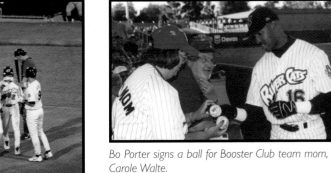

Bo Porter signs a ball for Booster Club team mom, Carole Walte.

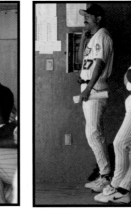

A.J. Hinch surveys the action from the upper deck of the dugout.

"Dial 911!-" Pitching coach Rick Rodriguez calls the bullpen.

"How'd you like that, Skipper?"

Mario Encarnacion collects his thoughts away from the crowd.

Justin Miller ready to deliver heat.

Got anything left? We just sent our best reliever to Oakland.

Jose Ortiz, MVP: A fighter.

Steve Decker checks for a sign from the dugout.

Roberto Vaz takes time to sign a few balls before the game.

Eric Byrnes steals 2nd base.

Decker unloads a grand slam against the Salt Lake Buzz!

Familiar? The River Cats were 48-19 at Raley Field.

Coach Roy White greets guests on Fan Appreciation Night.

All-Star 2nd baseman Jose Ortiz listens to coach Roy White.

A.J. Hinch on a rare day off.

A.J. Hinch coaches first keeping Mario Valdez close.

Mario Encarnacion has a few words with the media on Fan Appreciation Night.

Hinch nails an Iowa Cub in a close play at the plate.

Most fans never saw the River Cats' road uniform.

Adam Piatt talks with a reporter before the game.

Versatile Eric Martins was a valuable part of the River Cats infield in 2000.

Rodriguez and Justin Miller have a heart-to-heart.

Ortiz drills another homer!

Mark Bellhorn signs autographs before the game.

Lefty Jeff Kubenka delivers some heat.

Rich DeLucia gets some tips out in the pen.

A.J. Hinch gets on base.

Bob Geren and Jorge Velandia talking strategy at third.

Mario Valdez came from Salt Lake on a trade.

Eric Byrnes was a favorite of all the girls.

Mario Encarnacion sends one over the fence.

Jose Ortiz makes a young fan happy with an autograph.

Paul Sorrento signs autographs for a bunch of adoring kids.

From the corner to the dugout—Brunson makes the trek.

Bo Porter is welcomed back to the dugout after slugging a homer.

Jose Ortiz pleases kids with his autograph.

On deck, Vaz swings hard so hard, the moon

Sinks suddenly under the body of the ziggurat

Flaring like gold in the late, western sun, the jungle rumbles

With monkeys and tigers whispering in his ear, swing, Vaz, swing!

Vaz pulls back and picks up another heavy bat for balance

Holding them together like dangerous clubs for the sacrifice

Swinging a figure-eight over his neck, you can hear his back crack

In the ceremony on the sacrificial deck where one may walk

Or stones may fly in a powerful movement that flutters the flags—

The dead air of summer suddenly whizzing like a nest of dragonflies

All around him, thousands of people make ballpark talk

Their common voice smooth as grandmother's sweet corn

by Viola Weinberg

Vaz On Deck with the Gods

But in the head of Vaz, the Aztecs let blood run, taking their place to pull

To the mighty roll of the Sacramento at his feet, all groaning

In the mud brown, dangerous big moody, his lucky river

He will run like the river, through fields and across the valley floor

When he comes to bat, Vaz is fluid, swings this time for real

A devastating twist of flesh and bone, bulging with the blue veins

Of the good try, a swing so hard, his back ripples deeply—bang!

The ball climbs violently, bird of the gods, going, going, going, gone

River Cats Game-By-Game   April 2000

Day	Date	Opp	Outcome		Quickie Game Recap/Highlights/Notes
Thr.	4/6	@Fre	L	10-4	Cats stumble out of gate as Mulder gets shelled early as Grizzlies maul Cats.
Fri.	4/7	@Fre	W	12-3	Sac avenges previous night's thrashing with furious offensive attack.
Sat.	4/8	@Fre	W	10-9	Cats continue to pour on offense; Hinch raps four hits and mates belt four homers, three doubles and need every bit to finish Grizzlies who rally for five in the ninth. Porter joins Sac from A's.
Sun.	4/9	@Fre	W	11-2	Encarnacion explodes for homer and seven rbi; sparks Cats third straight scoring barrage as Sac rips Grizzlies again. Martins goes on DL.
Mon.	4/10	@Tac	W	2-1 (10)	After homer spree in Fresno, Cats kept in the yard, but Porter has game-winning rbi in 10th to provide difference in Sac's fourth straight win.
Tue.	4/11	@Tac	W	12-3	Mulder returns to normal dominant self while Piatt takes care of the run support with grand slam to highlight 4-hit, 5-rbi performance as Cats rattle 14-hits.
Wed.	4/12	@Tac	W	10-7	Number nine hitter Vaz hits pair of homers and drives in five; sparks Sac's sixth straight victory.
Thr.	4/13	TRAVEL/OFF DAY			
Fri.	4/14	@SLC	L	8-4	Six hits between Long and Piatt not enough to prevent Buzz from riddling Zito, snapping Sac's win skein; Cats now 6-2.
Sat.	4/15	@SLC	W	3-1	Strong pitching from five Sac hurlers and timely hitting help Cats pounce back into win column.
Sun.	4/16	@SLC	L	2-0	Sac generates only five hits while getting blanked by three Buzz hurlers.
Mon.	4/17	@SLC	L	14-6	Sac tries to slug with Buzz, get decked by 12-hit, 3-homer barrage.
Tue.	4/18	*Cgy	L	12-4	Home away from home: Raley Field still unfinished; Cats journey to Oakland to play first scheduled homestand on A's home field in Network Associates Coliseum before meager crowd of 2,188 including 1000+ bussed from Capital area; Sac spikes Cannons with 18-hit assault
Wed.	4/19	*Cgy	L	7-3	Long rips two doubles, but Zito gets roughed up and Sac drops opener of twin bill before 2,027.
		*Cgy	W	1-0	Sauveur wheels and deals and Porter drives in game's only run in 6th as Cats salvage doubleheader split.
Thr.	4/20	*Cgy	L	7-4	Cannons roar too loud for Cats, but Sac still holds top spot in Southern Division.
Fri.	4/21	TRAVEL/OFF DAY			
Sat.	4/22	@SLC	L	8-3	Cats gather 13 hits but leave 10 on base; fall to 9-7 but hold on to 1st place.
Sun.	4/23	@SLC	L	7-6	Sac's late rally to tie in 9th not enough to prevent third straight loss.
Mon.	4/24	@SLC	L	12-5	Jones shelled early as Sac road skid continues despite homers from Ardoin and Ortiz.
Tue.	4/25	@SLC	L	5-4	With Long and Piatt elevated to A's, Cats sign ML vets Sorrento and DeLucia, but suffer season-high fifth straight setback.
Wed.	4/26	@ SLC	W	10-5	Better late than never: Cats trail early, finally break out 'Buzz Saw' to cut SLC with 7-run outburst in 9th and salvage final game of tough 5-game series; Kubenka and Giambi join Cats.
Thr.	4/27	@Alb	W	7-6	Cats score seven runs on just six hits, as Porter drives in Giambi with decisive run in ninth.
Fri.	4/28	@Alb	W	10-5	Giambi and Bellhorn equally split 8-hits; spark 14-hit attack and lead Sac to third straight win. Cats now 12-10, one-and-a-half games back of leader.
Sat.	4/29	@Alb	W	6-4	Jones bounces back from shaky performance and Cats drill four doubles to highlight 12-hit flurry to lead fourth straight win.
Sun.	4/30	@Alb	L	15-12	Cats turn up offense and rattle 17 hits, but so do Dukes as Sac continues marathon road trip with tough loss in long slugfest.

*River Cats home games scheduled for Raley Field; played at Networks Associates Coliseum/Oakland, April 18-20

Day	Date	Opp	Outcome	Quickie Game Recap/Highlights/Notes
Tue.	5/2	@CSp	W 9-2	11-hit attack, Zito's strong pitching spark Cats' fourth win in last five games.
Wed.	5/3	@CSp	L 5-4	Cats whack 13 hits, strand 11 and squander 4-1 lead; SkySox win in 9th, Sac falls two-and-a-half back.
Thr.	5/4	@CSp	W 8-4	Vets Sorrento and Velarde, youngsters Vaz and Hinch all smack 3 hits each to equal season-high 18 hit barrage as Cats score in six different innings. Giambi returns to A's.
Fri..	5/5	@Csp	W 17-5	Cats claw a run per hit while Sorrento, Hinch, and Ardoin all drive in three runs; Jones stays steady on the mound as Cats again rip Sky Sox.
Sat..	5/6	@Fre	W 12-2	Ortiz drives in four while Sorrento and Martins homer as Cats again showcase torrid offense and pull within a game-and-a-half of top spot in the division.
Sun.	5/7	@Fre	W 6-0	Zito sparkles with 6-inning no-hitter and bullpen preserves 1-hit shutout; Vaz drives in four runs during Cats' 6-run sixth, but Ortiz' 14-game hitting streak ends.
Mon.	5/8	@Fre	W 8-1	Kubenka and Gajkowski shut down Grizzlies while Porter pounds pair of homers.
Tue.	5/9	@Fre	W 9-5	Sac smacks 11 hits, hurlers fan 13; Cats leap into 1st place tie.
Wed .	5/10	TRAVEL/OFF DAY		
Thr.	5/11	@Tac	W 5-2	Winning streak hits seven as Cats rip 11 hits and remain tied for first.
Fri.	5/12	@Tac	L 3-1	Ortiz homers, but Zito works on short rest and Cats fall to Rainiers.
Sat.	5/13	@Tac	W 5-3	Vaz and Ardoin combine to drive in all Sac runs but Cats manage only 6 hits in opening game victory.
	5/13	@Tac	L 5-2	In game two, Cats gather only 3 hits; Ortiz homer prevents shutout, leaving Sac with doubleheader split.
Sun.	5/14	@Tac	L 2-0	Exhausted Cats get blanked but Sac posts remarkable 22-15 during the "Mother-of-all-roadtrips" and head home to brand new Raley Field in first place.
Mon.	5/15	Edm	L 2-1	Super storm and 2-1 setback cannot deject or disappoint capacity crowd, media members and dignitaries galore who pack Raley Field for rousing home opener as Triple-A baseball returns to capital city area for first time since 1976.
Tue.	5/16	Edm	L 3-1 (10)	Newest River Cat Menechino drills 3 hits but Sac strands 12 runners in non-support of tough-luck hurler Jones.
Wed.	5/17	Edm	W 9-4	Sorrento grand slam keys 6-run 1st as Sac leads wire-to-wire for first home field win; improves to 6-over .500; one game back of Vegas.
Thr.	5/18	Edm	L 15-1	Edmonton traps Cats, Sac pitching riddled with 15-hit, 15-run torrent.
Fri.	5/19	Fre	W 11-5	Cats return favor, shred Grizzlies with 16-hit rampage highlighted by 8-run first.
Sat.	5/20	Fre	W 2-0	Prieto sparkles for eight-and-a-third and Service completes shutout before sellout crowd.
Sun.	5/21	Fre	L 5-3	Heavy heat wave for rare daytime contest cannot prevent another sellout, but Cats bow to Grizzlies.
Mon.	5/22	Fre	W 4-1	Menechino homers, Cats score early and Zito tames Grizzlies again.
Tue.	5/23	@Tcn	L 6-5 (10)	Menechino homers for second straight game and Cats out-hit Sidewinders, but Sac falls in extra-innings to begin road trip in sweltering Arizona heat.
Wed.	5/24	@Tcn	L 10-6	Bellhorn and Sorrento homer, but DeLucia gets bombed as Sac stumbles again.
Thr.	5/25	@Tcn	W 5-4 (13)	Porter rescues Cats with 3-run shot in 9th to tie game enabling Sac to win in thirteenth.
Fri.	5/26	@Tcn	L 10-6	Porter moves to leadoff spot, drills three hits, but Tuscon drills Jones; Velandia joins Cats from A's.
Sat.	5/27	Tac	L 4-0	Long, tall Ryan Anderson throws zeroes for five as Cats get just three hits in sellout loss; Piatt and Vizcaino return from A's.
Sun.	5/28	Tac	W 5-4	Call-up Lockwood and vet Bellhorn deliver key hits and Ratliff out duels Cloude.
Mon.	5/29	Tac	W 2-1	Vets shine; Jaha rehabs 2-rbi and DeLucia wheels and deals Cats to squeaky win.
Tue.	5/30	Tac	W 2-1	Sac gets another masterpiece from Prieto and clutch hits from Sorrento and Lockwood to sneak by Tacoma again.
Wed.	5/31	Tac	L 3-2	Zito pitches well, but continued lack of support kills the River Cats.

Day	Date	Opp	Outcome	Quickie Game Recap/Highlights/Notes
Thr.	6/1	@Okl	L 5-4	Jones' strong outing and Porter's 3-run shot are wasted as Ruben Sierra's last-hurrah homer dooms Cats.
Fri.	6/2	@Okl	L 6-3	Three Sac errors and quiet offense spell loss for Cats.
Sat	6/3	@Okl	Postponed	Inclement weather forces Sunday doubleheader.
Sun.	6/4	@Okl	W 5-3	Sorrento homers and Cats get five runs to break mini-skid with win in opener.
	6/4	@Okl	W 9-7	Sac offense back: Hinch raps 3 hits as Cats complete DH sweep and leaves OKC with series split.
Mon.	6/5	Cal	W 7-3	Piatt returns from A's to drive in 3; Bellhorn and Ortiz add homers to potent Sac attack.
Tue.	6/6	Cal	W 10-9	Martins leads the way as Sac smacks 11 hits, hurlers fan 13; Cats vault into 1st place.
Wed.	6/7	Cal	W 9-4	Winning streak hits seven as Cats rip 11 hits (again) and remain tied for 1st place.
Thr.	6/8	Cal	W 9-4	Ratliff provides stellar long relief and Hinch collects four hits to spark Sac victory.
Fri.	6/9	Edm	W 3-2 (10)	DeLucia sparkles, Piatt homers to tie it in sixth; Bellhorn rips walk-off homer in tenth.
Sat.	6/10	Edm	W 3-1	Prieto pitches seven strong innings; Sorrento has 2-rbi double as Cats win eighth straight with just five hits.
Sun.	6/11	Edm	W 4-1	Zito continues mastery; works nearly untouchable six-plus, leading Sac to front-running win.
Mon.	6/12	Edm	W 5-4 (12)	Sac can do no wrong as winning streak hits season-high ten-straight.
Tue.	6/13	@Tcn	L 6-5	Bellhorn and Vaz homers cannot save riddled Ratliff; streak snapped and Sorrento retires.
Wed.	6/14	@Tcn	W 9-2	Bellhorn (grand slam) and Vaz homer again, spark 8-run 7th while DeLucia holds for impressive comeback win.
Thr.	6/15	@Tcn	L 16-4	Sac pitching pounded for 20 hits in loss; Byrnes replaces Sorrento; Zito named to All-Star Futures games.
Fri.	6/16	@Tcn	L 6-5	Rare Zito slip leads to Cats' third loss in a row, despite Bellhorn three hits (with homer).
Sat.	6/17	@NO	L 5-2	Bad weather spoils travel plans, Cats arrive late, trail early; score too little, too late.
Sun.	6/18	@NO	L 4-3	Zephyrs score twice in bottom of 9th; Cats drop fourth in a row and fifth of last six at midway point in season.
Mon.	6/19	@NO	W 6-1	DeLucia twirls another gem; Bellhorn doubles twice; McKay KOs NO with big 3-run blast to lift Sac.
Tue.	6/20	@NO	W 5-1	Bellhorn's three triples ties PCL record and Byrnes tags first homer with Cats; four Sac hurlers carry load in win.
Wed.	6/21	TRAVEL/OFF DAY		
Thr.	6/22	LV	W 3-0	Cats tied for top spot as Piatt blasts game-winning homer in bottom of 9th; Ortiz named to PCL All-Star team.
Fri.	6/23	LV	W 13-12 (12)	Sac prevails in back and forth, 5-hour slugfest, giving Cats sole possession of first place.
Sat.	6/24	LV	W 15-6	10-run first sparks Cats' fifth-straight win to move 15 games over .500; average attendance at home exceeds 11,000.
Sun.	6/25	LV	W 8-5	Twelfth consecutive home victory, capped by Porter's "Circus Catch" in 8th sends Cats on road with 3 game cushion.
Mon.	6/26	@Edm	L 5-3	Late Trappers HRs ensure wire-to-wire win, snapping Cats' six-game streak.
Tue.	6/27	@Edm	L 6-5	Bullpen folds, allows 5 runs in last 3 innings, handing gift win to Edmonton.
Wed.	6/28	@Edm	L 7-5	Pen collapses again, surrenders late lead as Cats drop third straight loss; Las Vegas wins 3 straight to tie for 1st.
Thr.	6/29	@Edm	L 5-4 (13)	Cats drop fourth straight, fall into 2nd after relievers yield 13 runs, 26 hits in just 11 innings of work, failing in three-straight save tries.
Fri.	6/30	@Cgy	W 8-6	Sac halts losing skid as offense (13 hits/3 HRs) has best outing in six games. Velandia's slick fielding and power spark badly needed win.

Day	Date	Opp	Outcome	Quickie Game Recap/Highlights/Notes
Sat.	7/1	@Cgy	L 4-1	Cats garner just five safeties, K 13 times; succumb to awesome Cannons pitching.
Sun.	7/2	@Cgy	W 3-1	Zito's strong pitching, hot hitting by Byrnes help return Sac to win column.
Mon.	7/3	@Cgy	L 8-6	Cats whack 16 hits in loss and drop six of eight up north; still lead Vegas by one game.
Tue.	7/4	Tac	L 4-3	9th-inning rally falls short; eighth sellout crowd sees River Cats drop Independence Day toughie.
Wed.	7/5	Tac	L 12-5	Three solo homers not enough as Sac stumbles agian; trail early, rally to get close late; then get bombed. 11.567 see Cats suffer eighth loss in last 10 games.
Thr.	7/6	Tac	W 4-3	Zito's four scoreless innings and two Sac home runs produce important victory.
Fri.	7/7	SLC	W 5-4	Prieto returns, hurls pearls as Cats blast three more homers and regain rhythm.
Sat.	7/8	SLC	W 3-2	Jones' strong pitching and two more homers propel Sac to third straight 1-run win
Sun.	7/9	SLC	W 18-2	Sac completes first half in grand fashion with fourth straight win and four-game lead in Southern Division. Bellhorn scores six times as Cats establish new team high in runs and hits while completing sweep of Salt Lake City.
ALL-STAR BREAK				Pacific Coast League vs. International League; Frontier Field, Rochester, N.Y.
Wed.	7/12	AAA All-Star Game		Ortiz represents Sac well: goes 2-for-5 with a double in 8-2 PCL win.
Thr.	7/13	Fre	W 7-4	Cats start 2nd half with impressive late comeback win with four in 8th; now four games up on Vegas.
Fri.	7/14	Fre	W 3-0	Zito baffles Grizzlies before Sacramento's ninth sellout crowd of the season.
Sat.	7/15	Fre	L 6-2	Fresno grand slam does-in River Cats before 10th sellout crowd despite strong competition from Olympic Trials, Monarchs WNBA Basketball and World Team Tennis.
Sun.	7/16	Fre	W 7-5	Late clutch hitting and four double plays key victory as Cats again match season-best 16 games above .500.
Mon.	7/17	@LV	L 6-2	Cats stumble in road opener; see Southern Division lead trimmed to two games.
Tue.	7/18	@LV	W 6-4	Cats take early lead and hold on to move 16 games over .500 and go 3-up on Las Vegas.
Wed.	7/19	@LV	W 13-8	Effective patchwork pitching rotation and 8-run 9th produce key win; now 17 over .500 and 4-up on Vegas.
Thr.	7/20	@LV	W 19-10	Sac wins third straight from Vegas; Bellhorn rips two homers and Cats extend lead to five games and hit season high .591 (59-41).
Fri.	7/21	Nsh	W 7-6	Cats score in bottom of 9th to win 5th straight; improve to .594.
Sat.	7/22	Nsh	L 6-4	Sac falls in 12 innings to snap four-game streak and halt Ortiz' 16-game hitting streak before 13,661 at Raley Field.
Sun.	7/23	Nsh	W 4-2	Cats hurlers hold the fort and Velandia's homer breaks tie as Sac swings back into the win column.
Mon.	7/24	Nsh	W 7-6	Tape measue shot by Byrnes and another Circus Catch by Porter key decisive 5-run 5th as Cats 20 games over .500
Wed.	7/26	Iowa	W 11-5	Ortiz smacks three hits and drives in four as Cats continue to claw their way to victories.
Thr.	7/27	Iowa	W 5-2	Velandia's three hits and strong patchwork pitching lift Cats to season-high nine game lead in Southern Division.
Fri.	7/28	Iowa	W 5-2	Ortiz blasts tape measure homer as Cats continue to pounce on oppostion.
Sat.	7/29	Iowa	W 5-3	Sac wins for 10th time in last 11 games before sellout crowd; now 66-42 (.613).
Sun.	7/30	@Edm	W 8-5	Sac continues roll, so does Byrnes: extends hit streak to 15 games as Cats claw Trappers.
Mon.	7/31	@Edm	W 10-3	Ortiz promoted to A's, Ardoin dealt to Twins, but Cats win eighth straight; now 68-42 (.618).

Day	Date	Opp	Outcome	Quickie Game Recap/Highlights/Notes
Tue.	8/1	@Edm	W 8-7	Gold-Glover Porter rescues Cats with 9th inning homer as Sac extends win streak to nine.
Wed.	8/2	@Edm	W 4-2	Sac completes Canadian sweep posting season-high 10th straight win, now 70-42 (.625).
Thr.	8/3	Tcn	L 9-8 (10)	Cats 33-11 at Raley Field after Sidewinders sidestep Sac in extra frame to snap 10-game streak.
Fri.	8/4	Tcn	W 4-3	Sac registers its 17th last-at-bat victory to subdue slithery Sidewinders; Ortiz returns to Cats.
Sat.	8/5	Tcn	W 4-2	Ortiz celebrates return to Sac with three hits including huge blast as Cats stretch lead to 16 games!
Sun.	8/6	Tcn	L 7-4	Ortiz powers out another homer but Cats can't overcome 7-0 deficit.
Mon.	8/7	Mem	L 3-2	River Cats lose late lead, drop back-to-back games for the first time since losing three straight July 3-5.
Tue.	8/8	Mem	L 7-0	Cats get shut down and held to just one hit by the PCL's top pitching staff.
Wed.	8/9	Mem	L 2-1	Despite three hits from Byrnes and another strong outing from Miller, Sac loses toughie after leading 1-0 entering 8th
Thr.	8/10	Mem	W 6-1	Ratliff's pitching and Velandia's timely 3-run homer lead Sac salvage to prevent sweep.
Fri.	8/11	@Cgy	L 12-4	Cannons roar with several salvos and slap Cats in road opener. Sac still 25 games over .500 and playing .603 ball.
Sat.	8/12	@Cgy	W 13-5	Sac returns favor, routs Calgary as newcomer Rusty Keith and two other Cats rip 3 hits each to spark spike of last place Cannons.
Sun.	8/13	@Cgy	W 9-1	Sauveur tosses gem while newcomer "King Kong" Keith continues batting assault to boost Cats lead to 11 games.
Mon.	8/14	@Cgy	W 7-4	Decker leads offense with 3 hits and Double-A call-up Miller continues impressive streak. Keith returns to Modesto.
Tue.	8/15	SLC	W 8-4	Bellhorn rips inside-the-park homer while Encarnacion and Ortiz clout circuit blasts in exciting slugfest with Buzz.
Wed.	8/16	SLC	W 7-3	Byrnes rips 5 hits; Porter continues Cats' homer barrage; Cats go to 30-over .500 (78-48) with fifth straight win.
Thr.	8/17	SLC	W 7-3	Red-hot Byrnes continues to sizzle; robs Buzz of homer with acrobatic circus catch; then clouts 3-run homer to cap 10x14 series.
Fri.	8/18	SLC	L 5-1	Buzz finally muffle Cats' bats, prevent sweep and re-claim top record in PCL.
Sat.	8/19	Oma	W 7-1	Miller dazzles again; Ortiz explodes for three hits with 2 HRs (including Slam) to drive in six as Cats get back on track.
Sun.	8/20	Oma	W 7-2	Porter's tape-measure blast to dead center sets tone for Cats' cruise, lifting Sac to another high-water mark of 34 over .500.
Mon.	8/21	Oma	L 7-5	Injured Ortiz sits out as Cats yield 4-3 lead and come up short against Golden Spikes.
Tue.	8/22	Oma	W 15-5	Byrnes promoted to A's and Ortiz out (thumb) but Cats flex claws, turn on power and blast 5 homers; clinch PCL Southern division crown before beginning final eight regular season games at Magical Raley Field.
Wed.	8/23	TRAVEL/OFF DAY		
Thr.	8/24	LV	W 6-5	Cats squander late lead before Ortiz drives home Porter with winning run on 2-out single in 9th!
Fri.	8/25	LV	L 5-3	Never-say-die Cats rally to tie in 8th, but fall in 9th.
Sat.	8/26	LV	W 9-6	Starter Ratliff called up to A's just before game time; Porter rips three hits and adds PCL leading 36th stolen base in TV win.
Sun.	8/27	LV	W 10-4	Cats score early and often as Ortiz raps four hits and Porter and Bellhorn whack back-to-back homers; Cats go 14 over .500.
Mon.	8/28	Tcn	W 4-0	Sac establishes new franchise record with 86th win, surpassing old mark set in 85 and equaled in 86 and 88.
Tue.	8/29	Tcn	W 8-3	Porter and Ortiz homer, Decker decks Tucson with grand slam; win 8th out of 10, to climb to 37 over .500.
Wed,	8/30	Tcn	L 6-5 (10)	Cats let one slip through their paws; squander 4-0 lead into 7th; Velandia traded to Mets, Hinch and Valdez elevated to A's, while McKay, Hart and Salazar fill ranks in Sac.
Thr.	8/31	Tcn	W 10-4	Cats score early and often to rip Sidewinders in front of new record crowd of 15,216 on Fan Appreciation Night; Cats top Memphis for best home attendance, log highest numbers in history of PCL, with new standard of 861,808 fans entering Raley Field.

Day	Date	Opp	Outcome	Quickie Game Recap/Highlights/Notes
Fri.	9/1	@LV	L 9-4	Sac swoons in Vegas road opener after emotional regular season finale at Raley Field.
Sat.	9/2	@LV	W 4-3	Sac back on beam; Porter spanks three hits and sub McKay delivers big hit in 9th; Cats again leap to 36 games above .500 and a sixteen and-a-half-game lead in the Southern Division.
Sun.	9/3	@LV	W 4-3	McKay delivers again; 8th inning double drives home winning run for second straight game; Cats improve to 90-53.
Mon.	9/4	@LV	L 8-4	Bellhorn tags team-high 24th homer but Cats drop regular season finale to finish with series split, 90-54 season mark, Southern Division crown, and 48-19 record at Magical Raley Field.

The Playoffs

The **River Cats** ended the regular season with a 90-54 record and a sixteen-and-a-half game margin in the Southern Division of the Pacific Coast League. The squad seemed invincible heading into the playoffs. Following a one day rest, the River Cats were back at **Raley Field**, to battle the **Salt Lake Buzz** in a five-game series.

Matt LaRose and his crew had the field looking its best, adorned with the red-white-and-blue PCL Playoff logo behind the plate and the rarely used River Cats logos along each baseline. The crowd was pumped up as it poured into Magical Raley Field for its first taste of baseball playoff action.

In a shocker, the River Cats dropped a 10-4 decision to the Buzz. Although the Cats blasted four solo home runs, the Buzz busted a 3-3 tie in the seventh with two homers, including a grand slam, to send Raley Field fans home stunned.

The following night, the River Cats lived up to their regular season form, pounding the Buzz 4-0, behind a masterful outing by Ariel Prieto. Bo Porter's big home run juiced the crowd and sent the River Cats off to Salt Lake with the series tied up.

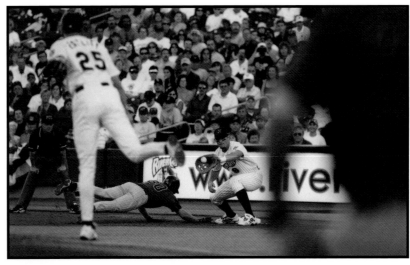

Game three in Salt Lake was a heartbreaker. After coming back twice from three-run deficits, the Cats lost a true nail-biter in the bottom of the ninth, as the never-say-die Buzz rallied to stun Sacramento again.

River Cats fans had no doubts that their team would be back at Raley Field for more baseball. In game four, the River Cats, behind the slugging of Jason Hart, scored early and often. A 10-6 Sacramento win forced the decisive fifth game the following day in Salt Lake.

Unfortunately, the well ran dry for the River Cats in Salt Lake City. Hammered early, the team came back to within one run in the seventh, but a huge rally by the Buzz in the eighth killed them and their season. Former River Cat Danny Ardoin helped seal Sacramento's fate with a huge series.

The Playoffs and the Sacramento River Cats' premiere season were suddenly over.

The Playoffs and Everything

by Viola Weinberg

O, to wake up again
And know nothing;
To neither waver at a thought
Nor stumble on a word
But to bathe in the shimmering bliss
Of unmeditated hopeful sensation—
Innocent of the odds
Simply gluttonous
In the cove of desire
Fires burning
In the appetite
Of that great and vacant
Reservoir of possibilities—
The lights blazing
And the doors open.

Ah, to wake up again
And puzzle over the whole thing:
Each ball of electricity
Distinct from the other
High blue plates of Autumn
Clacking against
The changing wind
The sky over the ballpark
Snapping with
Brisk white towels of clouds
On a high faint cloth of stars
A cold windy innocence
On the faraway diamond of earth
Where we knew nothing
And knew it all.

In memory of Father Larry Tozzeo

All the River Cats - All the Stats

PLAYER	AVG.	G	AB	R	H	2B	3B	HR	RBI	BB	SO	SB	CS	SLG.	OBP	E
Bellhorn, Mark, 3B	.266	117	436	111	116	17	11	24	73	94	121	20	5	.521	.399	19
Byrnes, Eric, OF	.333	67	243	55	81	23	1	9	47	31	30	12	5	.547	.410	2
Decker, Steve, 1B*	.272	62	243	22	66	12	0	4	43	34	40	1	2	.370	.356	3
Decker, Steve, 1B**	.284	110	405	51	115	23	1	12	78	74	62	1	2	.435	.393	10
Encarnacion, Mario, OF	.269	81	301	51	81	16	3	13	61	36	95	15	7	.472	.348	5
Espada, Josue, 2B	.234	40	145	21	34	7	0	0	10	27	23	7	2	.283	.356	8
Giambi, Jeremy, OF	.355	8	31	8	11	2	0	2	8	8	7	1	1	.613	.487	1
Hart, Jason., 1B	.278	5	18	4	5	1	0	1	4	3	7	0	0	.500	.381	0
Hinch, A. J., C	.266	109	417	65	111	23	2	6	47	45	67	5	5	.374	.344	4
Jaha, John, DH	.444	3	9	0	4	1	0	0	2	4	2	0	0	.556	.615	0
Keith, Rusty, OF	.500	4	16	5	8	4	0	2	6	2	2	0	0	1.125	.556	0
Lockwood, Mike, OF	.264	36	126	14	32	3	0	1	13	17	14	0	2	.302	.340	0
Long, Terrence, OF	.400	15	60	11	24	6	0	3	15	4	4	0	3	.650	.431	3
Marcinczyk, T.R., 1B	.231	11	39	4	9	1	0	1	3	4	7	0	0	.333	.318	3
Martins, Eric, 3B	.253	76	261	35	66	10	1	2	21	37	32	1	5	.322	.344	13
McKay, Cody, C	.224	16	58	8	13	4	0	1	7	5	14	0	0	.345	.297	1
Menechino, Frankie, SS	.316	9	38	8	12	2	0	2	2	5	4	1	0	.526	.395	0
Norton, Chris, 1B	.244	13	45	7	11	0	0	2	9	8	10	0	0	.378	.364	2
Ortiz, Jose, 2B	.351	131	518	107	182	34	5	24	108	47	64	22	9	.575	.408	32
Piatt, Adam, OF	.283	65	254	36	72	15	0	8	42	26	57	3	2	.437	.355	9
Porter, Bo, CF	.272	129	481	94	131	21	3	14	64	88	117	39	10	.416	.386	3
Rosario, Omar, OF	.296	8	27	4	8	1	0	0	1	2	5	0	0	.333	.367	1
Saenz, Olmedo, SS	.500	1	4	1	2	0	0	0	1	0	0	0	0	.500	.500	0
Salazar, Oscar, SS	.154	4	13	0	2	1	0	0	1	1	1	1	0	.231	.214	0
Sorrento, Paul, 1B	.278	40	139	25	38	9	1	6	32	33	34	1	0	.482	.406	0
Valdez, Mario, 1B*	.230	17	61	11	14	3	0	2	11	9	13	0	0	.377	.342	0
Valdez, Mario, 1B**	.344	105	378	87	130	27	1	20	96	66	59	1	1	.579	.441	5
Vaz, Roberto, OF	.289	114	426	56	123	22	3	10	72	49	72	20	6	.425	.362	3
Velandia, Jorge, SS	.278	83	302	56	84	20	1	9	57	34	52	4	3	.440	.369	11
Velarde, Randy, 2B	.455	3	11	3	5	0	0	0	2	4	2	0	0	.455	.625	0
All others	.278	0	234	42	65	16	1	6	34	34	72	6	0	.432	.385	23
Total–All Batters	**.285**	**0**	**4956**	**864**	**1410**	**274**	**32**	**152**	**796**	**691**	**968**	**161**	**67**	**.445**	**.375**	**142**

PLAYER	W – L	ERA	G	GS	CG	SHO	SV	IP	H	R	ER	HR	HB	BB	SO	WP	OPP AVG
Adkins, Jonathan	0 – 1	9.00	1	1	0	0	0	4.0	6	4	4	2	0	1	2	0	.333
Belitz, Todd	0 – 1	4.38	12	0	0	0	1	12.1	12	6	6	2	2	5	10	2	.267
Brunson, Will	3 – 0	3.65	18	0	0	0	0	24.2	26	12	10	0	1	11	22	0	.268
Burrows, Terry	0 – 1	1.38	2	2	1	0	0	13.0	8	2	2	1	1	4	7	0	.178
Corey, Bryan	8 – 3	4.24	47	6	0	0	4	85.0	28	43	40	11	3	29	55	2	.273
DeLucia, Rich	3 – 1	3.96	10	10	0	0	0	50.0	50	27	22	7	0	18	34	3	.259
Gajkowski, Steve	3 – 3	4.09	36	0	0	0	5	61.2	73	32	28	8	1	11	41	1	.298
Harville, Chad	5 – 3	4.50	53	0	0	0	9	64.0	53	35	32	8	3	35	77	8	.222
Jones, Marcus	6 – 4	4.35	17	17	0	0	0	101.1	108	57	49	7	2	36	51	3	.278
Kubenka, Jeff*	2 – 1	6.52	17	5	0	0	1	48.1	57	41	35	8	2	23	33	3	.294
Kubenka, Jeff**	2 – 3	6.55	21	5	0	0	1	57.2	67	48	42	9	3	29	39	3	.293
Kubinski, Tim	6 – 5	5.99	11	1	0	0	1	67.2	84	52	45	10	0	22	51	4	.299
Lankford, Frank	1 – 5	3.76	29	7	0	0	0	67.0	68	32	28	4	3	26	33	3	.269
Lehr, Charles	0 – 0	11.25	1	1	0	0	0	4.0	7	5	5	1	0	3	3	0	.389
Magnante, Mike	0 – 0	4.05	5	2	0	0	0	6.2	6	3	3	2	1	1	4	0	.240
Manwiller, Tim	1 – 2	6.49	5	5	0	0	0	26.1	34	23	19	6	0	12	22	0	.312
Mathews, T.J.	0 – 0	.000	3	1	0	0	0	3.2	2	1	0	0	1	1	5	2	.154
Miller, Justin	4 – 1	2.47	9	9	0	0	0	54.2	42	18	15	3	3	13	34	2	.210
Mohler, Mike	2 – 0	6.50	18	0	0	0	1	18.0	22	13	13	6	0	16	14	1	.297
Mulder, Mark	1 – 1	5.40	2	2	0	0	0	8.1	15	11	5	1	0	4	6	1	.375
Olivares, Omar	0 – 0	0.00	1	1	0	0	0	6.0	3	1	0	0	0	2	3	0	.158
Prieto, Ariel	8 – 4	3.27	20	18	0	0	0	113.0	110	51	41	9	1	31	79	4	.254
Ratliff, Jon	8 – 4	3.44	20	18	0	0	1	107.1	102	48	41	12	4	31	72	7	.254
Sanders, Scott*	4 – 3	6.52	10	7	0	0	0	49.2	63	36	36	9	1	13	38	2	.315
Sanders, Scott**	6 – 8	6.51	22	15	1	0	0	103.2	133	76	75	14	1	40	86	5	.317
Sauveur, Rich	5 – 2	4.57	25	11	0	0	1	82.2	88	48	42	7	1	25	59	0	.271
Service, Scott	6 – 2	1.30	33	0	0	0	13	41.2	27	8	6	1	0	11	50	5	.175
Snow, Bert	0 – 0	4.50	3	0	0	0	0	2.0	1	1	1	0	0	3	3	0	.143
Vizcaino, Luis	6 – 2	5.03	33	2	0	0	5	48.1	48	27	27	4	1	21	41	1	.276
Zito, Barry	9 – 5	3.19	18	18	0	0	0	101.2	88	44	36	4	2	45	91	5	.230
All others	0 – 0	0.00	0	0	0	0	0	0	0	0	0	0	0	0	0	0	.000
Total-All Pitchers	90 –54	4.16	144	0	1	6	42	1273.0	1291	681	588	133	36	452	940	59	.264

Artist Credits

COVER
"Baseball Comes Home"
Oil painting
Steve Barbaria

PAGE 1
"Berm and Bridge"
Pastel on paper
Carl Chiara

PAGE 2
"Sacto Flag 6"
Photographic construction
Bob Dahlquist

PAGE 3
"Ball Four"
Latex on wood panel
Mary Lynn Tenenbaum

PAGE 4
"Where was that pitch?"
Oil on paper
Stephanie Taylor

PAGE 5
"What's the score?"
Watercolor on paper
John W. Hansen

PAGES 6 - 7
"Baseball Comes Home"
Photo montage
Bob Androvich

PAGE 8
"Earl McNeely-Sacramento Solon"
Watercolor on paper
David K. Lobenberg

PAGE 9
"Edmonds Field"
Pen and ink on paper
Dan McAuliffe

PAGE 10
"Finally a Field"
Watercolor on paper
John W. Hansen

PAGE 11
"The Dream Team"
Photo montage
Bob Androvich

PAGE 19
"Where was that pitch?"
Oil on paper
Stephanie Taylor

PAGE 20
"The View"
Watercolor on paper
Lisa Carpenter

PAGES 22 - 23
"The Magic of Raley Field"
Photo montage
Bob Androvich

PAGE 28
"They Come to Games"
Watercolor on paper
John W. Hansen

PAGE 33
"Baseball Buffet"
Watercolor on paper
Mary Lynn Tenenbaum

PAGE 38
"Birds-Eye-View"
Watercolor on paper
Mary Lynn Tenenbaum

PAGE 42
"Safe at Third"
Watercolor on paper
Lisa Carpenter

PAGE 48
"Find the Ball"
Acrylic on canvas
Ed Weidner

PAGE 50
"The Duel"
Watercolor on paper
John W. Hansen

PAGE 63
"The Next Big One…"
Digitally altered photograph
Bob Androvich

PAGE 68
Cartoon
Ink and dyes on bristol board
Eric Decetis

PAGE 69
"River Cats"
Digital montage
Bill Prince

PAGES 70 - 71
"The River Cats Premier Season"
Photographic montage
Bob Androvich

PAGE 72
"Starting 5 and 9"
Acrylic on pitcher's rubber
Jolene Jessie (Sportraits)

PAGE 75
"Locker"
Pen, ink and watercolor on paper
Dan McAuliffe

PAGE 80
"Base Hit!"
Watercolor on paper
Mary Lynn Tenenbaum

PAGE 82
"Still Life"
Photograph
Gordon Lazzarone

PAGE 88
"Waiting for the Call"
Watercolor on paper
Lisa Carpenter

PAGE 90
"Meeting on the Mound"
Watercolor on paper
Mary Lynn Tenenbaum

PAGE 96
"Three Dog Night"
Oil on paper
Nan Roe

Photographic Credits

PAGE 4
Right field gate from Tower Bridge
Monica Turner

PAGE 5
River Cats pitcher
Bob Solorio

WE WOULD ALSO LIKE TO THANK THE FOLLOWING PEOPLE AND ORGANIZATIONS FOR THEIR HELP ••• CAL TRANS – LORING POLLOCK, MONICA TURNER, DURETTA MCNEELY, DICK BARLOW, TOM RUT, DALE TEMBROCK, AND MARTY LONGMIRE • BOB DAHLQUIST • ROBYN FULLUM • GRAPHIC CENTER – KIRBY STIVER AND THE MAC LAB • HOWE SPORTS INTERNATIONAL • IDEA FACTORY – BILL SWAN • SCOTT MARSH • MAGGIE MCGURK • OAKLAND A'S • PACIFIC COAST LEAGUE – BRANCH RICKEY, JR. • PARAGARY'S • JACK REEFER • RALEY'S – CHUCK COLLINGS, CAROLYN WHITE, JACK ALVAREZ • RAY REYES • RIO CITY CAFÉ – MICHAEL VAILLANCOURT • RIVER CATS BOOSTER CLUB – STEVE FRANKLIN • THE SACRAMENTO BEE • SACRAMENTO RIVER CATS: GARY ARTHUR, TONY ASARO, LIZ BROWN, PATSY COLEMAN, JACK DE GEORGE, DINGER, BRIAN FARLEY, DAREN GIBERSON, MIKE GAZDA, TOM GLICK, KRISTI GOLDBY, DARRIN GROSS, NINA HANDEN, DALE HAYNES, BOB (WHERE'RE THE NEGATIVES?) HERRFELDT, ESTHER LOPES, GREG MARQUITH, ARLOW MORELAND, GARY PHILLIPS, BRIAN THORNTON, DAN VISTICA, DAVE WOLLOCH • SAN FRANCISCO GIANTS – DUSTY BAKER • THE ZINFANDEL GRILL • JOIN THE CAT PACK...RIVER CITY BASEBALL BOOSTER CLUB ...P.O. BOX 417291...SACRAMENTO, CA 95841...FOR BOOSTER CLUB INFORMATION, CALL THE CAT PACK HOTLINE @ 916-732-4599 .

Opening night fireworks
Jim Lynn

Mario Encarnacion
Bob Solorio

Dinger
Jay Spooner

PAGE 12
Thomas P. Raley
Carolyn White of Raley's

Site - before
Beverly Walton

Site - Vision
John Tessler

PAGE 16
Sand Lot
Jay Spooner

PAGE 17
Turf is laid by the yard
Art Savage
Jay Spooner

I Did That!
J.R. Roberts
Bob Solorio

PAGE 18
Aerial photo
Tom Myers

PAGE 24
First fan
Jay Spooner

Gate from Tower Bridge
Monica Turner

PAGE 25
Tarp
Bob Solorio

Entrance
Ben Androvich

Hard-core fans
Jay Spooner

Rainbow
Jim Lynn

PAGE 26
Dinger and Bigwigs
Jay Spooner

Raley Field
Jim Lynn

PAGE 27
First "pitches"
Jay Spooner

Flying Old Glory
Jim Lynn

Dinger's entrance
Bob Solorio

PAGE 30
Kristi Goldby
Patsy Coleman
Finny Moseley
Jay Spooner

Diligent service
Bob Van Noy

PAGE 31
In-seat server
Lillian Townes
Friendly service
Bob Solorio

Val Mata
Tony Asaro
Toni Cordero

PAGE 36
Auto Mall
Bob Solorio

Beer Dawg - Steve Wall
Raffi on the 4th
Jay Spooner

"Krazy" George
Toni Cordero

Sacramento Bee carriers
Ostriches
Bob Solorio

PAGE 39
Bus and bridge
Toni Cordero

PAGE 40
Fireworks
Jim Lynn

Night shot from bridge
Fish eye lens
Jay Spooner

Fan's eye view
Bob Van Noy

Warm glow
Bill Prince

PAGE 41
Scoreboard
Fireworks
Jay Spooner

Darkness
Quiet Raley field
Bob Van Noy

Telephoto of berm
Bob Solorio

Night-time field
Bob Van Noy

PAGE 44
Night
Bob Van Noy

PAGE 45
Top left and top right
Jay Spooner

PAGE 46
Kids (both)
Toni Cordero

PAGE 51
Skyline
Bob Solorio

Tunnel
Bob Van Noy

PAGE 53
Fireworks
Jim Lynn

Tower Bridge
Jay Spooner

PAGE 54
Kid behind screen
Signing
Bob Solorio

Girls
Toni Cordero

PAGE 55
Future Oakland A
Jay Spooner

PAGE 56
Jolene Jessie
Kristy and Mike
Solons (both)
Bob Solorio

Jerry & Bill Oliver
Jay Spooner

PAGE 57
Gary & Phyllis Ordway
Jay Spooner

PAGE 58
Baseball is life…
Busfield Family
Jim Lynn

Mark Marvelli group…
Will James

Harry Devine
Girls
Solons
Bob Solorio

800,000th Fan
Toni Cordero

Hugging couple
Jay Spooner

PAGE 59
Cal fans
Vera Solorio
Woman with program
Bob Solorio

Chuck and Frances Collings
Maggie McGurk

Raley Field brought out…
Toni Cordero

PAGE 60
Joyce Diamond
Jay Spooner

Group on berm
Beerhead Sean Smith
Toni Cordero

PAGE 61
Bill Curren
M. and M. James
Toni Cordero

PAGE 65
Sunset (top)
Skyline
Bob Van Noy

Skyline (top right)
Bob Solorio

PAGE 69
A.J. Hinch
Bob Solorio

PAGE 76
Shadow ball
Bob Van Noy

Sorrento, Byrnes, Ortiz, Porter
Bob Solorio

Ortiz (slide), Zito
Jay Spooner

PAGE 77
High fives; Hinch; 911; Geren;
T.J. Mathews; Got anything?;
Decker, Decker, Familiar…
Bob Solorio

Encarnacion; Ortiz; Slide
Jay Spooner

PAGE 78
White and Ortiz; Hinch;
Rodriguez; Bellhorn;
Bob Solorio

Hinch the coach;
Hinch the tag;
Jay Spooner

PAGE 79
Lefty; Up from AA; Geren;
Encarnacion;
Bob Solorio

Ortiz signs; Valdez; Porter;
Jay Spooner

ALL OTHER PHOTOS
by Bob Androvich

IN A NEW STADIUM:
A Timeless Feeling
by Diana Griego-Erwin*

and

RALEY FIELD:
Just Right for Triple-A
by Mark Kreidler*

*©2000 Sacramento Bee
Originally published May 16th, 2000
Used with permission.

Missing The Magic

The awesome premiere season at Magical Raley Field has been over for almost a month. Fans—regular fans in particular—got hooked on the charm of the Raley Field experience during the first home stand May 15th through the 22nd. August, with three, eight-day home stands—separated by one four-game absence to Calgary and a single day-off—ensured fans remained deeply under the Magical Raley Field spell as summer faded to fall. The charm of the Raley Field experience, cast upon receptive visitors at 67 home games in just 109 days, was hard to shake.

The River Cats' sudden collapse and on-the-road departure from the playoffs in the first round ended the season without a real, final gathering of the faithful fans at their new home of baseball worship. The incredibly successful, magical, premiere season of the Sacramento River Cats at Raley Field was over, but without the chance to say goodbye, it never really ended.

Baseball had gone home. This time, though, it will leave only for the winter, to return home again next spring. So, on behalf of everyone at Magical Raley Field, we'd like to say, "See ya next year!"